Modern Psychometrics

International Library of Psychology

Modern Psychometrics
The science of psychological assessment

John Rust
and
Susan Golombok

R
ROUTLEDGE
London and New York

First published 1989 by Routledge
11 New Fetter Lane, London EC4P 4EE
29 West 35th Street, New York, NY 10001

Phototypeset in 10pt Times by
Mews Photosetting, Beckenham, Kent
Printed and bound in Great Britain by
Biddles Ltd, Guildford and King's Lynn

British Library Cataloguing in Publication Data

Rust, John
    Modern psychometrics : the science of
    psychological assessment. — (International
    library of psychology)
    1. Psychometrics
    I. Title II. Golombok, Susan III. Series
    152.8

Library of Congress Cataloging in Publication Data also available

ISBN 0-415-03058-7 (hbk)
ISBN 0-415-03059-5 (pbk)

To our parents

Contents

Contents

Tables and Figures

Preface

In the ten years following the race and IQ controversies of the early 1970s, psychometrics has been under consistent and widespread attack both within and outside psychology. Yet by the mid-1980s the extent of psychological testing in the USA and elsewhere was again on the increase. In this book we look at the underlying reasons for both of these phenomena and attempt a resolution.

In the early chapters we consider the role of sociobiology and its precursors on the development of the psychometrics movement and reach the conclusion that, although historically the relationship has been extensive, it is artificial. By defining psychometrics in terms of its utility it can be shown to be nothing more nor less than a very practical approach to what are very necessary aspects of the functioning of any society: selection and assessment. The major lesson of the troublesome sociobiological disputes of the 1970s is that selection and assessment are important social processes and thus the psychometrician cannot stand apart from ideological and political debate. In particular, psychometrics, if it is to fulfil its function of fair assessment and selection, must take a stand on issues of racism and injustice. This is particularly so in view of the overt racism of so many of its historical advocates.

The following chapters look at the practice and application of testing and test construction, paying particular attention to current issues such as the use of item response theory, criterion reference testing, profiling and minimum competency testing. Knowledge based tests of ability, aptitude and achievement are considered, as well as person based tests of personality, clinical symptoms, mood and attitude. The exceptional impact of the information technology revolution on all aspects of psychometrics is also examined.

The book is written in two parts. The first part deals with theoretical and more general issues in psychometrics. The second part is a step-by-step guide on how to construct psychometric questionnaires. This progresses through all the stages of test construction, from definition of the original purpose of the test to its eventual validation.

John Rust
Susan Golombok

Part one

Chapter one

The development of psychometrics

Definitions and origins

Psychometrics is defined in *Chambers Twentieth-Century Dictionary* as the 'branch of psychology dealing with measurable factors', but also as the 'occult power of defining the properties of things by mere contact'. While it is the first of these definitions that we shall be dealing with in this book, there have been times in recent years when the second might have seemed more accurate as a description of current practice, particularly in debates about intelligence. It is impossible to consider the development of modern-day psychometrics without looking at the substantial influence of the intelligence testing movement in the late nineteenth and twentieth centuries. However, the origins of the subject go back long before then.

Employers have assessed prospective workers since the beginnings of civilization, and in all probability have had consistent and replicable techniques for doing this. The earliest recorded examples of examinations for this purpose are from China at the time of Confucius, where there was a rigidly controlled and standardized system of examinations for the civil service. The pattern set down then — of a 'syllabus' of material which should be learned, and an 'examination' to test the attainment of this knowledge — has not changed in framework for 2,000 years and was in extensive use in Europe, Asia and Africa even before the industrial revolution.

The history of intelligence testing

Rapid scientific and social progress in Europe during the nineteenth century led to the development of several assessment techniques, most notably in the medical diagnosis of the mentally ill. However, the most dramatic impact was to come from a branch of pure science — biology. Darwin was the giant figure of the age, and his theory of evolution had considerable implications for the human sciences. In particular, his argument for the evolution of man by natural selection opened the door to human genetics based on evolutionary and biological precepts. In *The Descent of Man*, first published in 1871, Darwin argued that the intellectual and moral senses have been gradually perfected through natural selection, stating as evidence that 'at the present day, civilized nations are everywhere supplanting barbarous nations'.

Darwin's ideas of natural selection involved the intervening stages of 'the savage' and 'the lower races' at an inferior level of evolution to 'the civilized nations'. These ideas were, however, not introduced by Darwin but rather were his natural interpretation of prevailing opinion in England in the nineteenth century. They provided justification for colonialism and the class system, and served to maintain the British Empire.

The evolution of the human intellect was of particular interest to Sir Francis Galton, who in 1869 published *Hereditary Genius: An Inquiry into its Laws and Consequences*. Galton carried out a study of the genealogy of the famous scientific families of the time, and argued that genius, genetic in origin, was to be found in these families (which included his own). Thus we had at the end of the nineteenth century a popular scientific view, in accord with the philosophy and politics of England at that time, that evolutionary theory could be applied to man, and that the white, English, middle-class men of letters were at the peak of the human evolutionary tree. The hierarchical theory gave inferior genetic status to apes, 'savages', the races of the colonies, the Irish, and the English working class, and served as a justification for the social position of the dominant group.

Galton and the origins of psychometrics

Galton, a major proponent of this view, was the originator of psychometrics. He established an anthropometric laboratory at the South Kensington Exhibition in 1883, where persons attending the exhibition could have their faculties tested for threepence, and the data generated from this and other studies provided the raw material for the development of the tools of the trade. He also developed the twin study as a technique for looking at heredity, and together with his colleague, Karl

Pearson, developed the Pearson Product–Moment Correlation Coefficient for analysing these data. In fact, the attempts to measure intellect by these early tests were a failure, as very few of Galton's measures — visual, auditory and weight discrimination, threshold levels and other psychophysical variables — were particularly related to each other. However, the techniques and models of analysis still form the basis of present-day psychometrics. Galton also explored the idea of using the normal curve as a model for the distribution of test scores.

Pearson continued to develop the mathematics of correlation, adding partial and multiple correlation coefficients and the chi-square test to the repertoire of available techniques. Charles Spearman (1904), a former army officer turned psychologist, further developed procedures for the analysis of more complex correlation matrices and laid down the foundations of factor analysis. Thus by the first decade of the twentieth century the fundamentals of test theory were in place, and used almost entirely in the development of what had come to be called 'intelligence tests'.

What is intelligence?

The earliest pioneers in the area were generally unclear about what they meant by the concept of intelligence, and the question 'What is intelligence?' is still with us today. Galton effectively defined intelligence as that faculty which the genius has and the idiot has not. Herbert Spencer considered it to be 'the mental adjustment of internal relations to external relations'. Spearman emphasized school achievement in subjects such as Greek. It seems clear that these definitions have not arisen out of a scientific psychology but are extensions of the folk psychology of, if not the common man, the common school teacher. This psychology recognizes an important distinction between the educated person and the intelligent person. The former is someone who has benefited from a sound education. The latter is someone whose disposition is such that, were they to receive such an education, they would perform very well indeed. Whether a person receives such an education or not is very much a matter of social circumstance, so that a particular educated person is not necessarily intelligent, nor a particular intelligent person educated. Rather, the intelligent person was someone who could make the most of their education, and this was seen as part of the person's 'disposition'. Thus, intelligence was not education but educability. It was perceived as being part of a person's make-up, rather than socially determined, and by implication their genetic make-up. Intelligence when defined in this way is necessarily genetic in origin. Further underpinning for this approach came from psychiatry, where elementary tests were being developed to distinguish the insane from the imbecile, and as some of the various forms of mental defect were found to be due to genetic anomaly, so evidence was piled on presupposition.

Intelligence testing and education

Much of the early work on the measurement of the intellect was theoretical; however, applications were obvious and needs were pressing. In any society where opportunities for work or educational facilities are less than the demand, some form of selection is inevitable. If the job or educational programme is demanding in terms of the amount the applicant will need to learn before competency is reached, then there is an inclination to accept those who are seen as easier to teach, a task that could be simplified by testing for educability, or intelligence.

Alfred Binet was the first to provide an intelligence test specifically for educational selection. The main impetus came when the Minister of Public Instruction in Paris in 1904 appointed a committee to find a method that could separate mentally retarded from normal children in schools. Drawing from item types already developed, Binet put together a set of thirty scales which were standard, which were easy and quick to administer, and which effectively discriminated between children who were seen by teachers to be bright and children who were seen as dull, as well as between mentally retarded children in an institution and children in ordinary schools.

Following Galton and Cattell, psychophysical and sensory tests were known to be poorly related to educability, so Binet emphasized in his tests what he called the higher mental processes: the execution of simple commands, co-ordination, recognition, verbal knowledge, definitions, picture recognition, suggestibility, and the completion of sentences. The first scale was published in 1905, but an improved version came out in 1908 in which the tests were sorted into age levels, and in 1911 other improvements were made. Tests which might measure academic knowledge rather than intelligence — reading, writing, or tests of knowledge that had been incidentally acquired — were eliminated. The Binet tests and their derivatives (the Stanford-Binet in the USA and the Burt tests in the United Kingdom) were widely used throughout the world for the next sixty years for diagnosing mental retardation in children.

IQ tests and racism

From modern books on testing, what is supposed to happen to the children after diagnosis often seems unclear. However, this issue is particularly important to debates over streaming and separate schooling. There is an apparent confusion, probably ideologically based, between the idea that the bright children should not be held back by the dull, and the idea that the dull children should be given extra facilities to compensate for their disadvantage. However, older books are often more straightforward. The current sensitivity on these issues was not shared by the originators of psychometrics. Terman states in his introduction to the manual for the first Stanford-Binet (1919):

> It is safe to predict that in the near future intelligence tests will bring tens of thousands of . . . high-grade defectives under the surveillance and protection of society. This will ultimately result in the curtailing of the reproduction of feeble-mindedness and in the elimination of enormous amounts of crime, pauperism and industrial inefficiency. It is hardly necessary to emphasise that the high-grade cases, of the type now so frequently overlooked, are precisely the ones whose guardianship it is most important for the state to assume.

This view illustrates the close relationship between the development of academic and social interest in intelligence testing and concerns about human breeding before the Second World War. The Eugenics movement in particular was concerned about the dangers of the working classes reproducing more quickly than the middle classes, thereby lowering the average intelligence of the country. However, this interest in social engineering did not stop there: it also expressed itself in definitions of model humanity, the 'superman' in whom intellectual and moral superiority are combined. Thus Terman tells us, about children with high intelligence, that 'really serious faults are not common among them, they are nearly always socially adaptable, are sought after as playmates and companions, they are leaders far oftener than other children, and notwithstanding their many really superior qualities they are seldom vain or spoiled'. Compare this with Darwin in *The Descent of Man* (p. 126): 'The moral sense perhaps affords the best and highest distinction between man and the lower animals.' The intelligence testing movement at the beginning of this century was not simply like Nazism in its racialist aspects — it was its ideological progenitor.

Not all proponents were so extreme. Cyril Burt, who applied intelligence testing to school selection in England, was particularly concerned that the examination system was unfair to working-class children, and successfully argued for the introduction of intelligence tests in place of essays for the selection of children for grammar schools, on the grounds that the former would have less class bias. It has frequently been commented that when IQ tests were abolished for the eleven plus, the number of working-class children in grammar schools again decreased.

The Eugenics movement went out of favour following the Second World War, although by this time the ideas of intelligence which had been associated with the movement were fully ingrained in folk psychology. By drawing on a re-interpretation of popular ideas about mental defect, on a common interest in breeding and genealogy, and a widespread usage for selection in education and in the army, the various strands of belief had become mutually supporting to such an extent that many considered them to be self-evident. The use of the Binet scales continued, and the underlying ideological issues were resurrected by the sociobiologists, first Jensen, and then Eysenck, following an analysis of the performance of American black children in the Head Start programme. The aim of Head Start had been to counteract the adverse environmental conditions of black Americans by giving them an educational boost in their early years. Twin studies had shown that intelligence was about 50% inherited, and when the early analysis of the results of Head Start was negative, Jensen argued that the lower average IQ of American black people was due to a genetic difference between the black and white races. This was supported by Eysenck in his book, *Race and IQ*, who also extended the argument to the inheritance of intelligence in people of Irish extraction.

A heated controversy followed in which Kamin (1974) and many others attacked both the results of Jensen and Eysenck's experiments, and the ideological position of the intelligence testing movement which had led to this research being carried out. Kamin carried out a study by study critique of all the evidence for the inheritance of IQ scores and found it wanting. He did the same for studies which had purported to show differences in mean IQ score between racial groups. Following court cases in the USA, the most widely used intelligence tests in education were outlawed in many states, and testing generally came under increased scrutiny by the courts on the issue of cultural bias. While attempts were made to develop statistical models of alternative strategies to remedy any unfairness, such as positive discrimination (where selection processes explicitly favour members of a group which has been disadvantaged) and affirmative action programmes (where direct action is taken against the causes and cycles of disadvantage), the general disfavour into which psychometrics had fallen was widespread to such an extent that its teaching was downgraded or even eliminated in psychology and education courses throughout the world.

Issues in intelligence testing

Twin studies of intelligence

Paradoxically, however, by the mid-1980s, testing had become even more common than before. To understand why this happened we need to grasp the nettle which was evaded in the debates of the 1970s. The amount of data available now is so large that we can say confidently as a matter of fact that 50% of the variation in intelligence test scores is inherited. It is also a matter of fact that the mean scores of different racial groups on intelligence tests differ. However, neither of these results is as it seems and both need to be put into a proper perspective.

If we consider initially the genetic argument, the first issue of note is that in looking at twin studies we are dealing not with Mendelian genetics but with biometrical genetics. This difference is important because genetic results are generally interpreted by the man in the street in Mendelian terms, as taught in schools (for example, the inheritance of eye colour). The biometrical genetic technique has arisen more recently largely from agricultural engineering, where it is applied to the breeding of more productive species of plants and animals. One important difference between the Mendelian and the biometrical approach is that biometrical genetics deals not in absolutes (such as eye colour) but in the amount of variation in a particular trait. To see why this is important consider the theoretical effects of developing a perfectly equitable education such that every person received the same education. If this were the case there would be no environmental variance at all in educational level, which by default would become 100% genetic. Thus the more fair the educational system becomes, the more that variation in people will be determined by their birth. The fact that this perfectly straightforward aspect of biometrical genetics seems odd to us reflects the extent to which we are prone to misinterpret the results of this approach.

The form of surprise we feel with this failure of interpretation is demonstrated again when we look at the broader set of results in human twin studies. As more and more aspects of personality, ability and

9

performance are investigated under the twin model it is found that almost all psychological characteristics that we can reliably measure on human beings turn out to have both a genetic component and an environmental component, each accounting for about half of the variance! Now at once this raises an immediate exclamation: 'How interesting!', 'How amazing!', 'How remarkable that it should be about 50%!' Yet is it remarkable? Surely we have always known that much of our human identity is determined by our parents? Had the genes been different we could be apes, or fruit flies, or oak trees. It is common knowledge that many of our characteristics resemble those of our parents and close relations, and observations of family resemblance are made in primitive societies as well as in the modern world. The human personality exists in an exceptionally complex network, which draws not only on social and psychological factors but also on biology. All these aspects interact with each other and no aspects are independent. It seems as if a scientific confidence trick has been pulled. Common-sense knowledge has been quantified, translated into scientific jargon and served back to us as a justification for racism. But in spite of its technical format there is no new knowledge there — that is, unless we wish to follow up the technology of biometrical genetics and breed people in the manner we breed farmyard animals.

Societal differences in intelligence

In looking at the differences in mean IQ scores between different groups Jensen claimed that differences remained even when socio-economic factors were taken into account. However, the adjustment for cultural differences is no simple matter, and it seems implausible that these complex interaction effects can be adjusted for by any simple covariance analysis. Where different sub-groups within society hold differing relations to the power structure, it is the dominant group which defines the parameters by which things are to be judged, including the school curriculum. Generally speaking, members of a group which defines the standards perform higher on those standards, as was found, for example, in French Canada when the major language of instruction was changed from English to French. While previously the English-speaking Canadians had generally performed better than French-speaking Canadians in examinations, following the change this position was reversed.

The social movement of immigrants and other sub-groups in society is a matter for sociology rather than psychology, but clearly relates to the class and power structure in terms of the availability of resources, motivating factors for achievement, expectations of success and the perceived role of education. When one social group migrates to be within another, there is never a straightforward mixing of social equals. Many emigrant groups are driven out of their own countries by famine or persecution and arrive in the new society with nothing, and sometimes tend to be treated as nothing. Some groups emigrate to look for work, and will often find themselves at the bottom of the social structure in the new society, doing the jobs that natives refuse to do themselves. Other groups may have been driven out because of jealousy or political persecution, and may find a place for themselves in the new society providing skills for which there was a need. In all of these cases the tendency is often not towards absorption but to the development of sub-cultures. Members of these sub-cultures may, with luck, be free to compete for any advantages available to members of the society in which they find themselves. But it is unlikely that they will be quickly accepted into the groups of people who hold real power, that is, the power to say what counts as an advantage and to define the rules by which that society is controlled. It is those who hold this power within a society who also define what it means to behave 'intelligently' within it.

Test bias and test validity

In cross-cultural terms, differences in intelligence test scores have also been found between nations, with the Japanese apparently obtaining the highest scores. These types of result can often lead to some confusion among sociobiologists in Europe and the USA, but have been rationalized by suggesting that, although the Japanese may be better at simple problem solving, they probably are not so creative. This type of rationalization has also been used in the past whenever women have been found to have higher IQ scores than men on particular tests. Thus, according to Terman, while girls have higher scores overall than boys, the boys 'are decidedly better in arithmetical reasoning, giving differences between a president and a king, solving the form board, making change, reversing the hands of a clock, finding similarities, and solving the "induction test" '. The girls were 'superior in drawing designs from memory, aesthetic comparison, comparing objects from memory, answering the comprehension questions, repeating digits and sentences, tying a bow knot, and finding rhymes'. It is fairly easy to see here that all of the characteristics for

11

which boys are claimed to be better provide justifications for patriarchy, while the tasks at which girls excel are the ones more suitable for housework or secretarial work!

Wherever a difference between groups is found there is a choice of treating this as either evidence of bias or, alternatively, as evidence of validity, showing that the test is successful in measuring whatever it is supposed to measure. If we take social class as a case in point, there are well demonstrated differences between the social classes in mean IQ scores, with the professional class having the highest score and the unskilled manual class the lowest score. Now there is no a priori reason why this should not mean that IQ scores suffer from class bias. However, these results are never treated in this way. Rather there are aspects of the trait of intelligence as it is popularly understood which means that most people expect social class to be related to IQ. Thus, when it turns out to be so related, the result is treated as showing that the IQ test is valid. Whatever the IQ test is measuring, it is something which behaves as expected with respect to social class. But remember, statistics say nothing whatsoever about whether this is a case of validity as opposed to bias. Thus the distinction between these two concepts cannot be a statistical one.

If sex differences are now considered in the same light, we find that as attitudes to sexism have changed over the decades, so have attitudes to sex bias and validity in IQ tests. Thus, when Terman standardized his IQ scale and discovered that at certain ages girls were better than boys at certain sub-tests, he could have treated this as a scientific finding (girls actually are better than boys at these sub-tests), or as validity (girls were expected to be better than boys at these sub-tests; they are; therefore the test is valid), or as evidence of bias (this sub-test is biased against boys). In fact he chose the latter interpretation, and consequently changed the items until the scores for the two sexes were the same, a perfectly reasonable approach given the interpretation he chose to make. This all demonstrates the importance of social values in psychometrics, and that often the social positions which are taken for granted are the very ones we need to question in evaluating a test.

Intelligence and moral worth

The major rebuff for the sociobiologists on this issue must come from their definitions of intelligence. For sociobiologists, intelligence test scores reflect more than the mere ability to solve problems: they are related to Darwin's conception of 'survival of the fittest'. And fitness tends to be perceived in terms of images of human perfection. Generally speaking, if it was found that a particular intelligence test gave low scores to eminent scientists and artists this would not be seen as making a scientific discovery but as being overwhelming evidence that the test was invalid as a measure of intelligence. Intelligence as viewed from this perspective appears to be a general quality reflecting the person's moral and intellectual worth. The relation between moral qualities and intelligence is quite clear in the early biological literature, from Darwin and Galton to Terman and Burt. An important article in this respect was that of W.R. Greg in *Fraser's Magazine* (1868), which inspired a considerable debate. Part of Greg's claim is worth repeating, although offensive to some, because its combination of adjectives provides such an excellent example of the use of moral and intellectual factors interchangeably by supporters of this view. Greg claimed that:

> The careless, squalid, unaspiring Irishman multiplies like rabbits: the frugal, foreseeing, self-respecting, ambitious Scot, stern in his morality, spiritual in his faith, sagacious and disciplined in his intelligence, passes his best years in struggle, marries late and leaves few behind him.

This article was one of the main inspirations for the development of the Eugenics movement.

Spearman's 'g' or general factor of intelligence appears in his writings to have an almost spiritual quality. In *Human Ability* (1950) he speaks of a 'psychophysiological energy', which he compares to the basic theoretical concepts of physics (force, gravity, etc.). It is important to realize that here Spearman is not creating a new concept, but is making use of a very old and time-honoured metaphor. It is not entirely facetious to suggest that it is this same 'psychophysiological energy' which is thought of as providing the halo around the heads of religious saints or heroes. By using the metaphor in this way, Spearman generates an image of intelligence which represents not just the ability to answer simple arithmetical questions but also implies high moral standing.

The search for this single quality or essence of intelligence received much attention before the 1950s, although it was challenged by Thurstone and Guilford. Indeed we owe the origins of factor analysis as a statistical technique to this search. It became clear that whatever these tests were measuring did have some aspect in common, but what was not so clear was the extent to which this was dependent on a common educational system. Once a person receives an education, learns to read and to carry out arithmetic then all other sorts of learning become possible, so it would be very odd if, for example, ability at reading was not correlated with ability at languages or geography. But for the sociobiologist the existence of biological intelligence seems so self-evident that it takes precedence over common educational sense in providing an interpretation for experimental results.

The sociobiological view of intelligence

Another implicit assumption within traditional approaches to intelligence is the idea that the ability to solve a problem is based on the person possessing efficient basic information processing components within the brain. Thus, to be good at arithmetic a person would need to have not just a good memory for the previous steps in the calculation, but more specifically a good short-term memory for numbers. Tests of digit span are designed to measure this component. The subject is given lists of randomly ordered digits of lengths between four and thirteen, and after an interval of a few seconds asked to repeat them back. Most people can repeat lists of about seven such digits quite easily but find difficulty with ten digits or more. This test is easy to administer both forwards and backwards (with backwards digit span a person would have to repeat the digits in reverse order to that in which they were presented), and we would probably expect people who use numbers frequently to have longer digit spans of this type. But the interpretation of the test has often gone further than this. It is not seen as merely a measure of a skill but as a manner of gaining direct access to the brain component which carries out numerical memory. It has been assumed that unless this brain component is working properly a person cannot expect to be a mathematician. There is the further implication that the component, being within the brain, is part of our biology, and therefore of our genes. Other item clusters within intelligence tests attempted to measure other such components, such as the ability to recognize objects from different angles, to rearrange images of objects in the mind, or to recognize the basic logical relationships defined within symbolic logic. All this carried the implication that these basic skills must exist before a person can possibly proceed to any higher or more complex level of knowledge, such as reading or arithmetic. However, the ordering of the hierarchy in this way is not self-evident but a product of a particular rather mechanical view of how the brain functions. Why, for example, should a particular digit span be a prerequisite for being good at arithmetic? Is it not equally plausible that good mathematicians develop longer digit span through practice?

Eysenck and his colleagues at the Institute of Psychiatry in London perhaps provide one of the best illustrations of the thinking of socio-biologists about the nature of intelligence. They have carried out experiments to attempt to relate scores on IQ tests directly to brain functioning. Thus, for example, Hendrickson (1982) found that more intelligent individuals tended to have shorter latency for certain components within the EEG evoked potential response. This response is a very small change in voltage at the surface of the brain measured by an electroencephalograph, the same type of machine used to measure the more well known brain alpha rhythm. Unlike alpha, the evoked potential occurs specifically after the subject has received a sensory stimulus, such as an auditory 'beep'. The response only lasts for about half a second, and is an oscillation with several peaks and troughs. It is, however, very easy to measure because the responses to a large number of stimuli can be averaged. This eliminates any background effects (such as the alpha rhythm) and, if measured over about a hundred stimuli, produces a characteristic response which varies from situation to situation as well as from subject to subject.

The interest of the Eysenck school in the results of these experiments is based on the belief in the possibility of a direct relationship between a person's intellectual ability and the speed at which the neurones within the brain actually transmit nerve signals. This would be questioned by those who view intelligence as only having meaning within social, linguistic or ontological settings. Another supporter of the Eysenck approach, Alan Hendrickson, has also suggested that more intelligent people have faster synapses and more efficient RNA. In fact many of these results have been subsequently discredited (Rust 1976). However, they are of particular interest in that they demonstrate a particular way of thinking about intelligence. All of these results exist within a purportedly scientific framework, that of theory production, opera-tionalization and empirical testing. Very few of the individuals involved question the presupposition that the only real explanation of intelligence is a biological one, so that their aim is not so much to prove such a link but to find out the why and the how. The biology in this sociobiology is of the extreme reductionist variety; to such an extent that the eventual explanation of all human activity in terms of neurone activity is not seen as an empirical matter but as an a priori truth.

15

Intelligence and cognitive science

The general picture of the great, good and intelligent man, being, as if by right, at the pinnacle of evolution, has recently been dealt a considerable blow by the development of cognitive science. As cognitive science grew in the 1950s, several models of human performance were put forward based on computer models, and generally these emphasized the single channel information processing aspect of both the computer and human cognition. Information was shifted about and sorted by short- and long-term memory buffers and by various sorts of filter until it activated behaviour. However, these early models soon proved to be inadequate. First because they failed to take heed of the enormous amount of representational activity that takes place in the computer software, and second because they implied that the limits on human performance are set by the extreme difficulty of carrying out advanced operations like remembering and filtering. Yet ability to remember soon became an easy task for computers, and it was hard to see, given the complexity of the nervous system, why the brain should find it difficult. Seen from the cognitive science perspective it becomes much more difficult to explain why people forget, rather than why people remember. Soon the possibility of the fifth generation computer, one which is able to use language to read, write, talk and think, undermined any physical or biological reason for there to be only a single channel in the brain. Parallel processing computers are many times more powerful than single processor machines. Recent evidence from neuroscience suggests that the brain itself, to the extent that it can be treated as a computational machine, is far more complex and more massively parallel than any existing man-made computer (Rummelhart and McClelland 1986). Consequently, any limitations on brain performance are not very likely to be due to lack of information processing power.

At the same time experiments on human cognition were beginning to show that people generally are rather bad at carrying out intelligent operations. The work of Johnson-Laird, and Tversky and Kahneman, has shown that on the whole people get many simple logical and probability exercises wrong, while even simple computers are able to get them right. By the 1980s the 'complex' activity of arithmetic, seen as higher-order reasoning within intelligence tests, became available to children on calculators for less than five pounds. Increasingly, the development of expert knowledge based systems demonstrated that many of the skills of intelligent experts were fairly easily modelled on small personal computers. Paradoxically, it was the lower-order activities of perception and motor control which proved much more difficult to model. While it can be argued that just because computers can do something does not necessarily make it easy, a comparison of the complexity of existing computers with the very much more complex structure of the brain does suggest that mechanical limitations of this sort are not the apparently self-evident source of human intellectual limitation they once were.

This debunking of the traditional notion of intelligence is an ongoing process, and its eventual impact is yet to be determined. However, one side effect must be to elevate the worth of every human individual and to discredit any justification of wealth and power based on the abilities of some humans to simulate rather simple computers. The knowledge now available within information science is enough to render absurd the notion that the quality of mind arises from our ability to do simple logic, arithmetic and other basic operations of the type measured in IQ tests.

New models of intelligence

The new models of intelligence can be exemplified by the work of Robert Sternberg (Sternberg 1982). He puts forward a componential model of intelligence, based on information processing. The component is put forward as the basic construct for the understanding of intelligence, and is defined as an elementary process that operates on internal representations of objects or symbols. Thus, when a person sees an object, the sensory input is translated by such a component into a conceptual representation in the mind. Components are of numerous different types and exist at several levels. Sternberg defines five major kinds of component: metacomponents, performance components, acquisition components, retention components, and transfer components. Metacomponents are responsible for higher-order reasoning, they integrate components at lower levels and have a special role in planning out the steps for problem solving. Performance components are involved whenever a planned course of action is instantiated, including the processing of steps within a problem solving task. Acquisition components are activated whenever new learning is involved. Retention components are involved in the act of recall or remembering, but also generally wherever information of any type is searched for in the long-term memory. Transfer components are involved when generalization takes place, either transfer of training or the operation of the metaphorical process.

Sternberg's components are seen as having three major qualities: duration, difficulty and probability of execution. It is this very specific and operational definition of the component which enables the theory to be tested. By comparing the duration of different tasks, and the frequency of particular responses, the different componential steps in problem solving can be delimited, identified and examined. When examined within this framework many of the classical items of intelligence tests, such as pattern matching or block design, open up into a rich source of data for intelligence theorists. It is of particular interest that when the items are treated in this way, the superficially higher-order computational aspects of reasoning (calculation and verbal processes) are lesser problems than the need to understand more basic processes such as perception, intuition, and motivation. Sternberg's model and its successors enable us to study intelligence in a far more interesting way than by making gross comparisons between the performance of people.

The ethics of IQ testing

Intelligence tests certainly measure something, and this something is highly correlated with academic achievement. But the question 'What is intelligence?' may have been approached from the wrong direction. It is necessary to look more seriously at an alternative explanation: that educational achievement may be determining intelligence rather than the other way round. Within this alternative context it may be that, rather than a child being good at reading and good at arithmetic because of a high IQ, it is because the child is good at reading that he does better at arithmetic, and vice versa, the two learning processes being mutually supportive. Thus the core items of intelligence tests may be derivative rather than determining. When intelligence is viewed through the perspective of education, a natural relationship falls into place between the learning process and the achievement of intellectual skills. It seems natural to propose that the higher the educational achievement, the better one becomes through practice at simple intellectual tasks. The integration within computerized knowledge systems of instruction, understanding, learning and assessment is currently leading to a revolution in our understanding of the intellectual expert.

However, this is not a satisfactory place to leave the matter. It would be improper to suggest that the only reasons for attempting to eliminate racism within psychometrics was its factual inaccuracy. Many people would overlook the racism of Darwin and his followers on the grounds that most white people of those times knew no better. It would certainly be a mistake to let the matter detract from Darwin's other achievements. But these arguments cannot be accepted in their entirety, as this would be a disservice to those who, even then, were involved in attempts to eliminate racism. The litigation that individuals in many countries have had to take through the courts, the Civil Rights campaign in the American South, and the campaign by the Indian National Congress for the rights of the 'untouchables', to name but a few, all demonstrate that the matters of principle which arise within psychometrics cannot simply be treated as matters of empirical verification within science. The fight against the abuses of intelligence testing forms an integral part of the movement for more social responsibility in science, and also demonstrates that science is but a part of human life and cannot stand outside it. While science can develop our understanding, and can help us to predict and control the world, it cannot interpret our findings for us, or tell us how the world should be. Some people may believe that the worth of human beings is an empirical point; that the study of human genetics and the related disciplines is the job of an impartial scientist who must never be held back in his task for any reason, carrying out for us that special human endeavour: the search for truth. But this absolutist view does not generally hold, and much of what is true scientifically may have more to do with the discipline of engineering than pure science. There is, after all, a difference between the search for the true nature of the atom, and the search for the ideal design for an atomic bomb. Biometrical genetics is an engineering process, designed for the breeding of improved species, and does not necessarily have any relevance to psychology. On the other hand the belief in the equality of all human beings in terms of moral worth is an old one, enshrined in many world religions, and for most people it comes first. No approach which attempts to challenge this basic human belief can expect to be above criticism, and it is quite apparent that the concept of intelligence used by some psychometricians represents more than the straightforward ability to solve problems: judgments of human worth are also implicit.

The limitations of IQ tests

IQ tests have had their day in psychology and in society in general. They have had their uses, particularly in selection, but this has unfortunately been accompanied by gross unfairness. While the employer or the selection board that has used IQ tests may well have obtained good candidates, they will also have had a biased set of candidates, and the bias will reflect the patterns of injustice which already exist within the society. Consequently, any differences will be exacerbated, and unfairness will increase. Exceptions do exist, as for example when Burt introduced the IQ test as an alternative to written tests for English school selection. But this is a particularly interesting case in point, which very well illustrates the major dilemma of IQ testing. The previous written examinations were certainly more biased against working-class children than were the IQ tests, yet in spite of this eventually proved to be more socially acceptable. Why? Because a written examination doesn't basically claim any more than the ability to identify the child's learning. If the child does badly then there is always another chance to make good any learning which had been incomplete. The IQ test on the other hand is specifically designed to get at that part of the child's ability which is least affected by the child's learning — the child's innate potential. To obtain a low score on such a test is damning, and IQ tests exist not within a purely scientific realm of operational definitions but within a world where the term 'intelligence' is already heavily loaded with meaning. Society generally is unlikely to accept a system which condemns children at an early age to a life of low expectations, by both themselves and others.

Summary

Psychometrics itself has suffered considerable damage from the whole controversy about intelligence testing, but it is now time for urgent remedial action. The use of other forms of psychometric test is increasing in society, and it is important that all issues associated with this phenomenon are properly and objectively evaluated if we wish procedures to be efficient and fair. Many, of course, believe that there should be no testing at all, but this is based on a misunderstanding that has arisen from attempting to separate the process and instrumentation of testing from its function. It is the function of testing that is determining its use, and this function derives from the need in any society to select and assess individuals within it. Given that selection and assessment exist, it is important that that be carried out as properly as possible, and that they be studied and understood. Psychometrics can be defined as the science of this selection and evaluation process in human beings. But in this day and age we must realize that the ethics, ideology and politics of this selection and assessment are as much an integral part of psychometrics as are statistics and psychology. This arises in particular because any science dealing with selection is also by default dealing with rejection, and is therefore intrinsically political.

It is essential that psychometrics be understood in this way if we wish to apply proper standards and control to the current expansion in test use, and if we wish to develop a more equitable society. It is one matter to eliminate IQ tests, it is quite another to question the psychometric concepts of reliability and validity on the grounds that these were developed by eugenicists. It would be just as irrational to dismiss the theory of evolution and consequently most of modern biology! The techniques developed by Darwin, Galton, Spearman and their followers have in fact made a major contribution to our understanding of the principles of psychometrics, and it is to these matters that we now turn.

Chapter two

The objectives of testing and assessment

Psychometrics and sociobiology

Arguments about the ideological nature of psychometrics have traditionally been seen as one of a kind with arguments about sociobiology. Modern-day sociobiology has developed from social Darwinism, and has been most clearly described by E.O. Wilson (1975). Wilson's arguments span a wide area, and cover most aspects of contemporary society. The essential thesis, however, states that most of the social and political activity of modern man is but a reformulation of the activities of our ancestors. Collecting money on the stock market, for example, is seen as nothing more than the modern version of the berry collecting activity of our cave dwelling ancestors. The fact that women do not receive equal treatment in society is seen as being due to their natural disposition, as with their animal ancestors, to look after the home and children. Further, the thesis states that these continued social habits are not merely the result of tradition but a direct projection of human genetic make-up. There follows the implication that these traditional social practices are natural and unavoidable. Women should not expect to be treated equally in work, as that is not their natural place; the genes so decree! Now clearly there is a relationship between this sociobiology and politics, and of course, as we could expect, those political elements which support the status quo have found an ally in sociobiology. The connection of scientific sociobiological views with the far political right has led more radical scientists and politicians to condemn them out of hand as being politically motivated. However, most of the scientific proponents argue that they are not right wing at all, that they have merely, as scientists, stood back to look at the facts and these (sociobiological) facts are what they have found to be true. They will often turn the argument on their accusers at this point, equating them with those in Nazi Germany and Stalinist Russia who burnt books and locked up scientists rather than face up to the cold light of scientific truth.

The political and polemical public controversies on sociobiology and its pop psychological offspring, including the supposed natural inferiority of women and racial differences in IQ, do need to be looked at from a more disinterested viewpoint. First of all it should be obvious that a trap has been set, which has some similarities with that found when attempting to deal with the activities of the fringe religions. The ingredients are these: sociobiology is not just a science but a science with profound implications for society; the arguments in its favour are complicated and often involve a fairly sophisticated understanding of mathematical genetics; only those with career aspirations within the area are likely to have time to develop the skills necessary to understand these arguments, and to do any necessary experiments; there is no point in doing any of this unless you already believe in sociobiology. It might be useful to make a comparison here with some of the wilder fringe ideas, such as 'God was a spaceman', or 'the originators of Christianity were members of a hallucinogenic mushroom cult'. In all these cases the sceptic is confronted by a very impressive amount of evidence prepared by a believer or believers. Yet does the scientific method decree that he or she is obliged to go through all of this evidence and disprove the thesis? Such an exercise would probably take years, and by post hoc selection of evidence, very plausible cases can often be made for any queer idea. This is of course a 'no win' situation: unless you believe the hypothesis there is no point in wasting any time on it, yet unless such time is spent by a non-believer the counter evidence may never be gathered and put forward. Now both of these examples don't really matter, as there are (usually) not that many consequences that follow from various people believing that God was a spaceman; but the consequences that follow from encouraging people to believe that women are genetically inferior are immense.

Even though it is not very scientifically rewarding to spend one's scientific life criticizing the theories of others rather than building one's own, there are those, such as Kamin (1974), who have taken the plunge. However, this straightforward critical approach has two major flaws. First, there is the tendency to be over-critical to such an extent that some credibility is lost, as for example in the perhaps over-strenuous efforts to do down the results of twin studies, particularly when we know that for genetic variation in physical characteristics they are so self-evidently appropriate. Second, such an approach is in the end doomed to failure: the supporters of the approach can always produce new data, or selectively report old data, and as long as there are those who want to believe, a superficially convincing argument can always be made. Most people after all are not scientists, and when two scientists disagree, people tend to choose the side they like best. With so many people finding that their interests are served by supporting the status quo, sociobiology is assured of an indefinite market.

In fact, much more effective attacks on sociobiology have been made by philosophers (e.g. Kitcher 1985). The arguments here are several, but perhaps can be summarized by a simple observation: if human beings can fly, and build computers, why should they not be able to plan other aspects of their lives as they like? There are presumably no genes which predispose us to build these mechanical artifacts. The major difference between human beings and all other animals (and birds) is that there is the possibility of transcending genetic limitations. We could, if we wished, choose only to travel by foot, on the grounds that this was the only form of transport that our genes had allowed, or we could choose to keep our diseased appendix as our genes must have had a reason to put it there. Society can choose, if it so wishes, to keep women as house servants. But in all these cases we and society can also choose otherwise.

Is psychometrics a science?

Much of the controversy surrounding sociobiology concerns psychology, and in particular psychometrics. One approach to psychometrics, that of trait measurement, discussed later in this chapter, has been very much quoted by psychobiologists. The investigation of the genetic properties of the measured trait of intelligence, IQ, is one of their major interests. This area has been particularly prone to the use of the defence, 'We are but honest scientists doing our job.' If this were genuine science then they would have a strong case, but some may doubt whether pure science is the appropriate description for this type of work. Perhaps theories of psychogenetic engineering should, like theories in nuclear engineering, be more socially accountable. Certainly a stronger social view has been taken on human embryo cloning, where claims of 'pure' science can perhaps be made more strongly than for psychometrics.

Is psychometrics pure science, or is it applied science? Within the physical sciences it is relatively easy to distinguish the pure from the applied aspects of a subject. Thus, for example, in nuclear physics that research which concentrates on the nature of elementary particles is justifiable on the grounds that it extends human understanding, while research on the appropriate grade of plutonium for giving the best nuclear explosion is either unjustified or justified on grounds of national defence. To put it bluntly, the first is science, the second engineering. With psychology there are also those who study the subject academically, and those who are more interested in applications. However, we cannot necessarily define all academic psychology as pure science. Unlike, for example, the physical or chemical sciences, there is not consensus on the fundamental unit of psychology. Behaviour (or more particularly the stimulus and the response) have traditionally been put forward, and more latterly 'information' has become a candidate. In *Philosophical Investigations* (1972) Wittgenstein summed the matter up: 'The confusion and barrenness of psychology is not to be explained by calling it a "young science"; its state is not comparable with that of physics, for instance, in its beginnings. For in psychology there are experimental methods and *conceptual confusion.*' This observation still holds true today. It is not so much that no psychology is scientific but rather that the scientific approaches of the different psychological schools are often inconsistent, with the advocates of each putting forward their own as the solitary genuine example. The trait approach to psychometrics is one such school and shares this characteristic. Thus while trait psychometricians may assume that they are the true and only proponents of the subject, this is still a matter of opinion. Trait psychometrics is only axiomatically true if sociobiology is axiomatically true, and this is widely disputed. Further, this argument can be extended to all other measured psychological traits as well. To put it at its most basic: are IQ, neuroticism, or attitudes entities worthy of understanding in their own right, or are they measured merely because of the need to make decisions about individuals, and thus simply artifacts of social policy.

Within (and outside) psychometrics there are proponents of both of these views. Trait psychometricians argue that the psychological traits their tests measure are very real, and are subjects of interest in their own right, while functional psychometricians argue that psychometrics can only be judged in terms of the success or failure of its applications. Both approaches have had their successes and failures. However, as with many such apparently clear-cut dichotomies in science, neither the theory nor the practice of psychometrics is this simple. To have a proper understanding of psychometrics as it is today we need to draw on different aspects of each.

What does psychometrics measure?

Psychological and educational tests carry out a form of measurement but, unlike physical measures such as length or weight, there is considerable confusion over what they measure and how they are able to do so. One particular problem is that what is measured is not a physical object but is an intervening construct or a hypothetical entity. In assessing whether a test of creativity, for example, is actually measuring 'creativity' we cannot compare a person's score on the test directly with his or her actual creativity. We are restricted to seeing how the test scores differentiate between creative and non-creative individuals according to some other ideas about how creative people should behave. The measurement of concepts like creativity or intelligence is limited by the clarity with which we are able to define the meaning of these constructs, and this has been a problem for intelligence tests in particular. Within the intelligence testing debate the facetious definition of intelligence as being merely that which is measured by intelligence tests has often been quoted with approval. However, intelligence tests must be measuring more than this, as otherwise they would not of necessity correlate with anything. But what more are they measuring? In attempting to answer this question it must be recognized that the problems encountered here are conceptual rather than scientific in nature.

Two models of psychometrics: trait and function

The way in which the subject matter of psychometrics is defined divides the two psychometric schools: the trait and the functional. Both these schools are further divided by their underlying philosophies. For the functionalist school the source of the discipline is seen as lying within occupational and educational testing, particularly the examination system. Within the strict functionalist approach, the design of a test is completely determined by its use, and 'what it measures' has no meaning other than this application. The simple paradigm for test construction provided by the functional psychometric model gives a definition of purpose, a breakdown of the areas relevant to the purpose in terms of, for example, a job specification or educational curriculum or psychiatric diagnostic procedure, and the design of a test specification based on this task specification. The test specification, or test blueprint as it is often called, is normally two dimensional with a content axis and a manifestation axis, and provides a regulated framework for the choice of test items. This simple paradigm can be applied to almost all assessment and evaluation situations, whether they involve interview or objective test, continuous or final assessment, single test scores or profiles, or personality, achievement or competency testing. It is the one used in the second part of this book.

Functional test design

The major contribution of the functional model to recent psychometrics has been the increased emphasis on test design. Planning frameworks formerly used within educational curriculum design are now generally applied across a whole spectrum of testing situations. The basic model has been the traditional two-dimensional structure of the curriculum, with one axis for content areas of instruction and the other axis representing different manifestations of the content areas. As an example consider the possible design of a test following the completion of a school geography syllabus. This might include a number of content areas such as map reading, political geography, geology, and trade, while manifestations may include skills such as having a knowledge of the terms used, understanding the subject, being able to generalize the knowledge, and the application of the knowledge within novel situations. These skills, and variations on them, are based on systems for devising objectives in educational settings (Bloom 1956). The two category systems (that is, content area and manifestation) can provide a two-dimensional grid with the four content areas representing the x axis and the four manifestations the y axis. The purpose of this grid is to enable us to find a predetermined number of items for each of the sixteen cells which exist within this 4×4 matrix. Thus, as long as the original test specification reflected the balance in the curriculum, so the test items should reflect this same balance. In most tests both axes generally include between four and seven categories. However, this has not come about because all tests have by nature a two-by-two design with from four to seven categories in each. On the contrary there is no implicit a priori rule which says we cannot have, say, five dimensions or thirty-seven categories. Rather, use of this type of test specification has arisen by convention because it has been found to be effective. Humans do not work comfortably with more than three dimensions, and two can be more easily represented. Also, given the desired length of the average test and the time constraints on its administration, more than seven categories on either the horizontal or the vertical axis would generate too many items. On the other hand

with only one dimension, or with fewer than three categories, not enough
spread would be generated to cover adequately the purpose of the test.
There have been and will continue to be many tests where one or three
dimensions are appropriate, or where a considerable number of cells will
not be filled within a particular two-by-two structure, but these are
exceptions which exist within the framework provided by the conventional two-dimensional, four to seven category model.

Trait test design

Trait psychometrics arose originally from attempts to be more scientific
about common-sense notions of different types of human personality.
An important idea was that of the personality spectrum, suggesting that
types of personality were not 'all or none' but had many possibilities
between the extremes. Thus, for example, people were not entirely good
or entirely bad but their goodness or badness could be represented along
a continuum. Personality was all a matter of degree. The first person
to use this approach in a scientific way was probably Sir Francis Galton
(1869) in his attempt to define the essence of genius. Within the trait
approach, the basis of individual differences in personality is assumed
to be related to individual differences in the biology — whether
biochemical, physiological, anatomical or neurological — of the human
organism. Psychometric tests were thus devised to measure traits which
were seen as representing biological variation in personality or aptitude.

The two key sets of philosophical assumptions for this approach are
reductionism and determinism. While both of these assumptions are
complex and are prone to oversimplification, they do need to be
considered, as otherwise there is the danger that what is basically a
difference of approach will be seen as an empirical difference requiring
experimental evidence to prove the matter one way or the other. In fact
neither reductionism nor determinism is open to empirical proof: they
are a priori philosophical positions. Consider, for example, the a priori
position involved in the following dialogue. Person A: 'Only matters
that can be proved by evidence are scientific'; Person B: 'Can you prove
that?' (collapse of stout party). In the same way the proponent of
sociobiology does not require evidence to be sure that there is no such
thing as 'free will', or that all social and psychological science will
eventually in principle be explicable by biology. These seem to be self-
evidently true. Many trait psychometricians today continue to be
reductionist in outlook and to believe in the strong version of biological

determinism. However, we shall see later that there is no necessary connection between the trait model and these philosophical approaches. Superficially the functionalist and the trait model seem very different. However, they do have common aspects, their method of construction is similar, and in particular they are linked by a fundamental theorem of psychometrics: the theory of true scores, which is described below.

The theory of true scores

The theory of true scores states simply that any score on an item or a test by a subject can be represented by two component parts: the subject's true score on whatever the item measures, and some error of measurement. This is traditionally stated as:

$$X = T + E,$$

where X symbolizes the observed score, T symbolizes the true score, and E is the error. From this it is clear that if all one knows about a subject and a test is that a particular person obtained a score of X on a test, then one knows nothing at all. In these circumstances the error and true score are inextricably mixed. For example X may be 5, yet this could be the case if $T = 3$ and $E = 2$, but equally so if $T = 110$ and $E = -105$. Thus an observed score (X) on its own is of no use whatsoever. It is the true score (T) we are interested in, and we need additional data to find this; primarily we need some idea of the expected size of the error term (E). To put this another way, we cannot know how accurate a score is unless we have some idea of how inaccurate it is likely to be. The theory of true scores takes us through various techniques for obtaining an idea of the size of the error (E). This is done by the process of replication, both by taking more measurements on the same subjects, and by measuring observed scores on different subjects. In deriving the theory of true scores from these data, several additional assumptions have to be made, and these are known as the 'assumptions of the theory of true scores'.

The first is the assumption that all errors are random and normally distributed. This is not particularly controversial as error, by definition, is random and, so long as the scaling factors are appropriate, error will be distributed normally. The normal curve is itself derived from the theory of error. The second assumption is that the true scores $(T's)$ are uncorrelated with the errors $(E's)$. This can be rather more problematic. There are circumstances under which the assumption fails, particularly where larger errors are associated with low, high or generally extreme scores, but these deviations are all adjustable (in principle at least) by various algebraic transformations of the raw data. The third assumption is that different measures of X on the same subject are statistically independent of each other. This is rarely true in the strict sense as the estimation of error is not usually very accurate, and the concept of error itself is open to interpretation (see the later discussion of reliability in Chapter 5). The net effects of breeches of this assumption blur the distinctive nature of the true score itself. Thus there will be some variation in the size of the measured true score depending on the particular way in which the error is estimated.

If the three assumptions of true score theory are made, then a series of very simple equations falls into our lap. These equations produce a measurement of error such that when a particular characteristic of a test is known — its reliability — we can determine the error and thus estimate the true score. (For a simple description of the mathematical derivation of the classical psychometric statistics from the theory of true scores, see Ferguson's (1981) *Statistical Analysis in Psychology and Education*. For a complete and rigorous statistical treatment of all the assumptions and derivations of the theory of true scores, see Lord and Novick's (1968) *Statistical Theories of Mental Test Scores*.) Although the theory has been widely criticized and many attempts have been made to improve it, the alternatives are generally complicated and usually turn out to have flaws of their own. After almost a century, the theory of true scores continues to provide the backbone of psychometrics.

Criticisms of the theory of true scores

The major criticisms have been directed against the concept of the true score itself. It has been argued that there can be no such thing as a true score, as this is merely a hypothetical entity generated by the theory (Loevinger 1957). This is the essence of the 'intelligence is merely what intelligence tests measure' standpoint. It is argued that we cannot deduce from a score on a test that anything whatsoever 'exists' in the brain, as intelligence is a construct arising from the use of the test. The true score as such is seen as being mystical and therefore of no theoretical importance. The response to this criticism has been to differentiate two definitions of true score: the Platonic (Sutcliffe 1965) and the statistical (Carnap 1962). While each of these will be seen to have its respective strengths and weaknesses, it is possible to support the theory of true scores by the statistical definition alone, so we will consider this first.

The statistical true score

The statistical definition defines a true score as being that score which we would obtain if we were to take an infinite number of measures of the observed score on the same person and average them. As the number of observations approaches infinity, then the errors, being random by definition, cancel each other out and leave us with a pure measure of the true score. Of course it is not possible to take an infinite number of measures of X on the same person, or often even one hundred such measures, without changing the measuring process itself because of the respondent's perceptions of the situation, practice effects, and so on. But this is unimportant from the point of view of the statistical definition, which states that the true score is the score which we would obtain *were* this possible. There is no need to actually do it.

The Platonic true score

The Platonic concept of a true score is based on Plato's theory of truth. He believed that if anything can be thought about, and the unicorn is often given as an example here, then even if it does not exist in the world, it must exist somewhere if such a thought is to be possible. Non-existence is reserved for objects about which we cannot even think. The Platonic idea of the true score is generally held to be a mistake (Thorndike 1964), with the implication that psychometricians who argue for the existence of a construct from the existence of reliable test scores make a category error. Just as behaviourists argue that there is no 'mind' only behaviour, so, it is said, there is no 'true score', only a series of observed scores and deductions. However, this is probably an oversimplification. There are many abstract nouns in use which, although not attached directly to objects, certainly exist: for example 'justice' or 'misery'. Certainly, in one sense, we might agree that justice and misery do not physically exist, but we would probably not see this as being equivalent to agreeing with the statement 'There is no justice in the world' or 'There is no such thing as misery.' Just because an abstract object has no physical existence it does not mean that it cannot be of any use, or indeed that it is not an object, unless we wish to indulge in semantic quibbling.

The true psychometrics: trait or function?

A particular importance of the statistical definition of the theory of true

31

scores is that it enables the theory to support functionalist as well as trait based psychometrics. For example, if we have a selection task of 'getting the best person for a job', then we can define the true scores on the selection test as 'those the use of which would select the best person for the job'. Trait psychometrics, while supported by both the statistical and the Platonic definitions, does tend to be more Platonic in its demands, and for many trait related tests used in psychology a statistical definition of a true score on its own is probably inadequate. A scale which sets out to measure the level of someone's depression presumes that misery exists in some sense other than the merely statistical.

The best example of the pure form of a functional test is perhaps given in the job-selection situation. In the construction of such a functional test the first task is to define the personality and skill requirements of a person carrying out the job in question, and this involves the drawing up of a carefully considered job description. Once this is done, the selection test uses an extension of this job description as its blueprint. If this process is properly conducted then the test score should give an estimate of a person's match to the job. In theoretical terms, if the test is purely functional then there is no need to build any psychological constructs into the situation. The test items can be specifically about the tasks the person will need to perform to carry out the job effectively.

Another area in which functional tests have been particularly useful is in educational assessment. Here the specification for the test can be based directly on the curriculum taught.

The 1970s in particular saw a shift away from trait based and towards functional psychometrics, largely under the influence of decisions made in the American courts on issues of test fairness. An example was the case of Griggs vs Duke Power Co. (1971), where a challenge to the use of a particular test for promotion purposes led to the court judgment that in employee selection, if racial discrimination is found as a result of using a specific test, then it is necessary for the user of the test to demonstrate its validity for the intended application. These matters will be considered in more detail in Chapter 6.

The functions of a test can be diverse. We may wish to select individuals for the Space programme, or we may wish to select students for university. We may not wish to select at all, but instead may be interested in identifying areas of weakness or strength in a student's performance in order to remedy defects in teaching. We may wish to test in order to evaluate teachers, or schools, or the curriculum itself. We may be interested in testing to feed back to a student information about his or her approach to learning, or we may wish to give a final score for the student at the end of a course to give some indication of what he or she has learned. This final score may be intended as a measure of the achievement of competency on particular skills, or of ability to develop further skills, or of both. We may wish to identify individuals with a particular disposition or motivation for a job, or for a course of treatment. We may work in a clinical setting and wish to determine which areas of the brain have been destroyed by a stroke, different brain areas being known to be associated with particular skills.

The functional approach is able to produce tests for all of these circumstances and many more, but it has one weakness: we cannot assume that a test developed with one particular purpose in mind will necessarily be of any use for another. In many areas of application, however, this has been seen as a strength of the model rather than a weakness. In education, for example, the separation of the function of formative assessment, where tests are used to identify areas of the curriculum which need to be developed by both teacher and pupil during the remainder of the educational session, and summative assessment, where a final indication of the pupil's attainment is given, has been widely welcomed. The way in which summative examinations control the curriculum has been widely criticized, and the formative assessment process welcomed as an approach which not only limits this control but also introduces feedback at a time when something can be done about it, rather than when it is too late. However, it still must be recognized that the actual content of both types of examination will be broadly similar, and in practice there will be considerable overlap between the content of each.

The functional model insists, almost as a point of principle, that no psychological intervening variables or traits can be relevant. As with behaviourism, the only interesting aspects of traits are the behaviour to which they lead, and as this is measured and defined directly and functionally, the traits are redundant. Within functionalism there is no such thing as, for example, ability in mathematics. There is only the performance of individuals on various mathematics items. There is, of course, much argument about the existence or otherwise of 'ability in mathematics' and the nature of such a concept. People do tend to use these concepts, and it is often on the basis of such concepts that generalization from a test score to an actual decision is made, whether justified or not. How else could an O level in mathematics, for example, be used by an employer in selecting a person for a job. Certainly it is unlikely that the mathematics syllabus was constructed with any knowledge of this employer's particular job in mind. Neither is it likely that solving simultaneous equations will actually be a skill called for in the job in question. Indeed how many people who have an O level in mathematics have ever 'found x' since leaving school? No, the criteria used in practice here are not functional ones but involve the use of folk psychological theorizing, and folk psychological constructs by employers. Many universities require successful applicants to be qualified in Latin for similar reasons. These examinations are seen as measuring folk psychological traits.

Thus we see that, in spite of the superficial advantages and objectives of the functionalist approach, trait psychology still cannot be eliminated while it so closely represents the way in which people actually make decisions in the real world. While it could be argued that all such trait related processes are wrong, and must be replaced by functionalism, this is probably an unreasonable and unwarranted idealism. It is really no good trying to prescribe human thought processes. To an extent much of psychometrics is no more than an attempt to be objective and consistent in predicting how people behave. If this can be achieved by assuming the existence of traits then so be it. Examples of the success of the approach abound, particularly in clinical psychology. A test of depression such as the Beck Depression Inventory (BDI) (Beck *et al*. 1961) although originally constructed around a framework defined by the functional model which identifies a blueprint of depressive behaviours and thoughts, would be of little use if it had to be reconstructed with each application of the concept of 'depression' in different circumstances. Functional tests on their own can only be specific to a particular situation, they cannot be generalized. If we wish to generalize then we need a concept, a trait of depression, to provide justification for saying that the depression scale might be applicable in changed situations, for example with children, or with reactive as well as endogenous depression. To function in this way the BDI needs to have construct validity, and this cannot exist without presupposing the construct and trait of depression itself. The process of construct validation will be considered in Chapter 5. The BDI relates to a wide range of mood changes, behaviours, thought and bodily symptoms which psychologists, psychiatrists and therapists consider to be part of depression. Paradoxically the decline of trait psychometrics in educational psychology has developed alongside an increase in its clinical use. Thus while the Wechsler Intelligence Scale for Children has declined in educational use and is now illegal in many American states, its cohort, the Wechsler Adult Intelligence Scale, has become the international standard for the assessment of intellectual deficit in adults.

These apparent paradoxes can be resolved if it is recognized that the application of psychometrics is itself a social process, and it is not so much a question of right and wrong as what is appropriate or inappropriate. What is appropriate for some circumstances can be inappropriate for others. Within this context the question of which of the two models, the functional or the trait, is scientifically correct becomes meaningless. Both are alternative techniques for dealing with the same underlying phenomena. Perhaps it would be illuminating here to consider parallels with the ways in which the medical model is used in psychiatry. Within this field there are many sets of symptoms which could be interpreted in different ways. For example, is bad spelling due to laziness or due to dyslexia? Or, is a particular instance of crime due to wickedness or to psychopathy? These types of issue are disingenuous as they give apparent alternative explanations with the implication that one must be correct and the other incorrect. However, the data are the same whichever model we take. The major distinction between the alternatives is not their correctness but the implications of accepting each. Thus if bad spelling is due to dyslexia, then an examination board may well consider that special exemptions are appropriate, which they would certainly not consider for laziness. Similarly, whether someone has been wicked or is ill determines whether they will go to prison or hospital. Here we can decide which of these two solutions is of most benefit to society. So with psychometrics, there is little point in arguing over which of functional or trait theory is correct, rather we need to consider the consequences of applying each.

What is particularly attractive about the functional model is its ability to map directly on to any selection or assessment process, so that justification for the use of a test is shifted to questions about the justification of the selection or the assessment itself. This makes sense, as it is here that the genuine ethical, ideological and political problems exist. The role of psychometrics should be to take within its scope the consideration of these issues, and first to justify the need for a test before proceeding to deal objectively with the achievement of the task in hand. It would then become the responsibility of the psychometrician to consider all aspects of any selection or assessment process, rather than simply the statistical or quantitative aspects of testing technology. This expansion in the scope of psychometrics which has taken place under the functional model has enabled psychometric test results to be seen within the same framework as other forms of functional assessment, such as the structured interview, the unstructured interview, and the general psychology of decision making. All lead to functional decisions and can be evaluated on the same objective functional criteria.

Traits, functions, and psychometric debates

The functional approach is also able to throw a fresh light on some of the traditional debates within psychometrics — for example, the argument about whether one factor or many are required to measure the construct of intelligence. Within functionalism, the deciding criterion is simply the use to which the test is to be put. Thus a test for selection must necessarily end with a mapping onto two categories, pass or fail. If 100 items are to be used within the test, then we would only want those items which contributed to the pass or fail decision. As there is only one way in which a scale with two effective final categories, that is our 'pass' or 'fail', can be divided, then by definition there is only one dimension appropriate for our test construction. This would have to apply even if the results of several sub-tests were being used in arriving at a decision. Here, weightings of the importance of each sub-test would be applied and summed to generate a score on the one scale necessary for making the pass or fail decision. Even if a manager simply makes a snap decision on the selection of an employee by judgment alone, a decision about what is relevant must have been made, a strategy must have been worked out for weighting these factors, and these must have been combined to produce the decision on a single two-point scale, accept or reject. In these circumstances the existence of only one scale, as opposed to several, turns out to be merely an artifact of the decision process in question, rather than an issue relating to the true nature of what was being measured. If on the other hand we look at assessment situations where no selection decision needs to be made — for example, a curriculum to be evaluated or the strengths and weaknesses of a particular learner to be assessed — then we would need to have a large number of different measures in order to produce an overall picture, and a single scale would be next to useless. Here we would construct a diversity of sub-scales. Although we may wish to know whether they are related, there would be no demand that they have any common element. These sub-tests would generally be presented as a profile, and examination of profiles of this type is very common where assessment rather than selection is the task in hand.

The functional model of the uni-dimensional nature of pass/fail decisions is particularly effective in practice. However, there are circumstances in which it breaks down, for example, where a judgment is made by a series of branching decision rules, e.g. if the person has X then do look at Y, if not look at Z, etc. The recent development of expert knowledge systems in cognitive science has given an alternative technique for investigating decisions of these types. The application of these expert systems within personnel and educational decision making has led to a rekindling of interest in the trait based model of psychometrics. When human experts are interviewed on how they make decisions about people, it is noticeable that much of their judgmental process is based on estimations of the person's personality and aptitude in general, and not on the very specific pieces of performance defined by the job specification itself.

Bridge building between trait and function

It is this focus on the actual thinking processes of the human decision maker which has built the bridge between functional and trait based psychometrics. Although, in principle, we can envisage a pure functional psychometrics in which everything in, for example, a selection test is based on what a person selected is expected to do, in fact, judgments about what is expected will be made by humans, and will be constrained by human psychology. These constraints will include the current classification and generalization systems of human folk psychology. Consider a parallel example. The need to reduce racial prejudice in society has occasionally led to the simplistic notion that it is possible to eliminate stereotyping altogether. Yet as soon as the realities of how people actually function are observed this becomes not so much an impossible as a meaningless task. Stereotyping has been shown by social psychologists to emerge from the need of individuals to make decisions in circumstances where data are inadequate. Thus when a person meets another for the first time, the only way to proceed is to work on the assumption that some of the person's characteristics are similar to those of people already known. It is difficult to imagine how humans could behave otherwise. The same applies with the folk psychological use of traits of personality and intelligence. These immediately become evident in practice when we look at how personnel experts trained in selection and counselling in fact identify the 'right person for the job'. The assessment of the intelligence and personality of others is a pre-existing part of human functioning within society. Although its mechanism is unknown, it reflects the behaviour of people as they actually are.

One valuable outcome of the recent ascendancy of the functional model in psychometrics has been the emphasis on obtaining a clear definition of the purpose of the assessment, and subsequently of the selection or assessment instrument. The initial definition of purpose should be simple and straightforward. A further outcome has been the increased emphasis on bringing the presuppositions and procedures for the construction of each test into the open so that they can be justified within the public domain. If the test is to be acceptable, to be seen as fair, and to be defensible in court, the purposes, once clearly formulated, need to incorporate adjustment for possible biases or irrelevances. Issues dealing with any specific requirements — for example, the need to recruit more women to a job to adjust for a traditional male bias — need to be incorporated into the rationale at this early stage. For example, men have been preferred as truck drivers on grounds of the physical strength needed for steering. This no longer applies with the advent of powered steering. Similarly, analysis of police recruitment procedures in the UK was found to discriminate unfairly against members of shorter races under the height rule. Unlike traditional trait based tests, functional tests do not make an artificial distinction between statistics (being the job of scientists and technicians), and issues of implementation (being the job of politicians and lawyers). All who are involved in the requisition, design and construction of functional tests need to integrate these societal issues into their practice at each stage of this procedure.

Summary

Both the functionalist and the trait approaches have their advantages and disadvantages. Neither can be said to be wholly right or wholly wrong. What is important is that psychometricians should realize which set of assumptions they are using in a particular situation, and be prepared to justify this use.

Chapter three

The process of test construction

Psychometric tests are composed of individual items, and the common characteristics of tests can more often than not be applied to individual items as well. Thus the simple question, 'Are you interested in this job?' can be scored (0 for yes and 1 for no, or vice versa), can be unreliable (that is, some people may give different answers each time), can be invalid (the answers may be wrong), or it can be biased (such as when some types of people may be more likely to lie than others). It can also be administered by interview, it can be judged by observation, or it can be tested by a paper and pencil multiple choice item (tick one box for 'yes', the other for 'no'). Although there are some cases where selection might be made purely on the basis of one question (e.g. 'What General Certificate of Education A levels do you have?'), this is unusual. More often there are many aspects we might wish to cover, especially as it is usually the case that the opportunity to ask one question provides an opportunity to ask many more. However, all tests are composed of individual items as their elements and so the success of a test depends on the success of its items.

Knowledge based and person based questionnaires

There are several important distinctions that are made between types of item, and these affect the tests which contain them. Items can be either knowledge based or person based. A knowledge based item is designed to find out whether a particular person knows a particular piece of information, and such tests measure ability, aptitude, and achievement. Most educational and intelligence tests are of this type as well as some clinical assessment instruments. A person-based test is designed to measure personality, clinical symptoms, mood or attitude. One major difference between these two types of test is that knowledge based tests are necessarily hierarchical and cumulative. The development of human knowledge moves in a particular direction from not knowing to knowing. Person based tests on the other hand carry no such implication. Different personalities and different attitudes are just different, and there is no intrinsic implication that to hold one attitude is necessarily better or worse, or more or less advanced, than the holding of another. A consequence of this difference is that the scoring of knowledge based items tends to be uni-dimensional, the person either gets the right or the wrong answer. The scoring of person based tests on the other hand can go in either direction. Thus someone with a low score on an extraversion scale would have a high score if the scale was reversed and redefined as an introversion scale.

Objective and open-ended tests

The objective test item

A second distinction between item types is between the objective and the open-ended. The major type of psychometric item in use is the objective item, so called because its scoring is entirely objective. These items are usually either true/false, or multiple choice. The first of these occurs when the respondent merely has to say whether a particular statement, e.g. 'The capital of Brazil is Rio de Janeiro', is true or false. The multiple choice objective item gives a number of choices (e.g. 'The capital of Brazil is (a) Rio de Janeiro, (b) Brasilia, (c) São Paulo, (d) Bahia') and the respondent has to choose only one of the several possible answers. Items of this type are called objective because the author decides in advance exactly what defines the correct response, and thereafter responses are marked right or wrong against this standard. Thus as soon as the respondent has placed his or her tick on the response sheet, the rest of the process is automatic and there is no room for error.

Comparing objective tests with essay tests

In educational settings, objective items of this type can be contrasted with the more traditional essay-type test, which is relatively open ended and therefore involves a certain amount of subjective judgment by the examiner in its marking. There are advantages and disadvantages in the use of both essay tests and objective tests and it can be instructive to compare them. It is often claimed that essay tests are able to measure originality, while objective tests are not. In fact this is probably an over-simplification. Originality itself, and creativity in particular, is in practice nearly always a matter of degree, particularly in education. Both the term originality and the term creativity turn out to be extremely difficult to pin down and operationalize in any application. Thus a 10 year old who thought out Einstein's theory of relativity from first principles would certainly be being creative, but not original as Einstein got there first! It is because of distinctions of this type that it is in fact possible to construct objective test items that can measure creativity reasonably well, in spite of the seeming paradox. The claim for the superior ability of the essay test in measuring originality is also open to question. In practice, truly original answers are not particularly likely to achieve high marks, especially if they are written as an alternative to showing a straightforward knowledge of the taught syllabus.

Objective tests are claimed to have advantages over essay tests in their ability to ignore extraneous factors. It has been demonstrated in several studies that it is very difficult for the marker of an essay to ignore spelling, grammatical and punctuation mistakes in a text, even after being instructed to do so. This seems to apply to experienced and inexperienced markers alike. However, while objective test enthusiasts often speak of the advantages of separating the qualities being measured, arguing that if spelling is of interest it should be tested separately, there are certain advantages in measuring the written abilities of the subject at the same time as the academic skills. In particular, if the subject will eventually need to be able to write reports of any form there can be an advantage in testing this knowledge in an essay.

One clear advantage of an objective test is its reliability of scoring. There are three ways in which different markers may vary in how they award marks. They may differ in terms of the average level of marks given — some markers prefer to award high marks, either because they feel generous or because this can sometimes cover up a lack of rigour in marking, while others tend to prefer giving low marks. Markers may also differ in the variability of their marks, and taken together these factors can have a large effect. Thus marker A may give marks out of 100 with a mean of 70 and a standard deviation of 20, ranging between marks of 100 and 5, while marker B may give a mean of 40 and a standard deviation of 5, ranging between 35 and 52. However, both these forms of difference can be eliminated by standardization (see Chapter 5), where means and standard deviations of the two sets of marks are equated. A more serious problem is lack of inter-marker reliability. Essay marks are well known for their unreliability, and even when different markers are carefully instructed in the different points to look out for in a particular essay, the correlation between their sets of marks is rarely above 0.6. There is no way of adjusting for discrepancies of this type. Time of day and the order in which scripts are marked are also known to affect the marks. Objective tests on the other hand should, by definition, have an inter-rater reliability of 1.0.

Another advantage of the objective type of item is that, by requiring all respondents to attempt all questions within the whole test specification, it is possible to obtain information about which material the respondent does not know as well as what he or she does know. Essay-type tests necessarily allow the respondents to choose for themselves which aspects of the answer are important, so that there is often the possibility of avoiding the direct revelation of ignorance. Because the objective test covers the whole test specification and therefore presumably the whole curriculum, it is usually quite easy to identify the relative strengths and weaknesses of respondents from their answers. However, we can set against this the fact that it is impossible to guess the right answer in an essay test but that this can be relatively easy in an objective test.

Finally, the two forms of test differ in their relative construction and marking times. The proper construction of an objective test can be a long drawn out process, with very careful consideration being necessary for defining the test blueprint, and the need for proper piloting. Essay questions on the other hand are relatively easy to set. When it comes to marking, these roles are reversed. Objective tests are very easy to mark, and in fact this process can now be done entirely mechanically, with optical scanners and computerized scoring. Essay marks, however, need individual human attention to be given to each script. The net effect of these differences is to favour essay tests where only a small number of candidates is involved. Here, the total amount of marking is small and the long time that would be required for constructing an objective test may not be justified. On the other hand where a test is given to a large number of respondents the particular strengths of the objective test are immediately obvious: it takes no longer to construct an objective test for 10 subjects than it does for 10,000 and while the marking of 10,000 essays would be a horrendous task, with an objective test this load can be taken over by a computer.

Open-ended tests in psychology

It is not only in education that open-ended psychometric items have been used. In psychology they have been suggested for use in creativity tests of the 'How many uses can you think of for a brick?' variety. Although an objective score can be defined in terms of the number of different responses, a subjective element creeps in whenever attempts are made to define 'different'. Thus 'To build a shop' and 'To build a church' should probably count as one response, but it is not really possible to define very precisely what counts as the same response. There is also a series of what are called projective tests in use in psychology, such as the Rorschach test, where the respondent has to report on what they see in an ink blot. Here again it is very difficult to be completely objective in the scoring.

Norm reference and criterion reference testing

Another important distinction has been made between items which are said to be norm referenced and items said to be criterion referenced. By far the major change which took place in psychometrics during the 1970s in the approach to constructing test items was due to issues surrounding this distinction. Until that time there had always been an emphasis on the need for psychometric test items to be selected in such a way that the test scores would have a normal distribution if administered to a large sample, and could be easily standardized. This achieved the aim of obtaining the maximum discrimination between individuals, and used the performance of the whole group of individuals as the standard against which each individual was judged. The response of a person on a test was then generally interpreted in terms of his or her relationship to the average. Although comparison against the norm can be useful, there are many situation where such comparisons are irrelevant, and where the peformance of the respondent would be more appropriately measured against some outside criterion. The work of Popham (1978) has been particularly important in the development of techniques for the construction of such criterion related items. Popham argued that there had been too much emphasis on normative factors in testing; that a normal distribution of test scores, and the purported need for as large a spread of scores as possible to obtain maximum discrimination between individuals had been over-emphasized at the expense of fulfilling the purpose of the test. He pointed out that if, for example, we are interested in whether someone

43

could ride a bicycle or not, then the performance of other people on their bicycles may well be irrelevant. Further, if we have a group of individuals, and wish to know whether they can ride bicycles, then we should be delighted if they all turn out to be able to do so, and not concerned that we do not have a wider spread of abilities. He suggested that there was no special need for the distribution of scores on a test to be normal. According to Popham, it is performance on the criterion which matters, even if all individuals obtain the same score.

When a test has been constructed with particular reference to performance on some objectively defined criterion it is said to be criterion referenced. When the major characteristic by which the score of a respondent on a test is judged is comparison with the whole population of respondents, it is said to be norm referenced. The issues raised by Popham led to a debate about the relative merits of norm referenced and criterion referenced testing. However, attempts to contrast norm and criterion referenced testing too strongly can be misleading, as the two approaches do have much in common. First, all items must be related to some criteria. Indeed, given that there is an intention that tests be valid, each item must relate to the purpose of the test itself. This purpose can only be judged in terms of criteria, and thus criterion referencing is a necessary aspect of validity for all tests, whether criterion or norm referenced. In fact, the situations in which it is possible to lay down strict single criteria for a task are extremely limited, and in practice the circumstances in which we are pleased if everyone gets 100% on a test are extremely unusual. This is not because people are less than delighted at success but rather that the only occasions in which this occurs seem to be those in which the information could probably be known with no testing at all. If we do go to the considerable task of constructing a classroom test we hope to gain some information from the results, and the conclusion from a 100% success rate is more often that the test, and perhaps the curriculum, were probably too easy rather than delight at the success of teacher and pupils. Some information on any difficulty the pupils had in mastering the material, or on what the teacher found difficult to present, would probably be more useful. If all of the many applicants for a single job were tested and shown to be equally good, we would of necessity need to question our criterion. Of course, there are many instances where all we wish to know is whether a particular person can do a particular task or not. But this situation is not one which stands apart from traditional psychometrics, it is rather a special case within it.

Why is it that classical psychometrics has looked for normal distributions across a population in test scores, and has used the properties of this distribution to derive its statistics? This has not arisen because the normal distribution has some magical properties, which psychometricians have insisted human beings must meet. The normal distribution needs some demystification. It merely represents the distribution to be expected when large numbers of random factors can influence the score, and is indeed derived directly from probability theory. In any selection or evaluation processes error is always present to some extent, and if we wish to understand the performance of data in the presence of error, we must be able to quantify it. The estimation of error is made very much easier in situations where the data are normally distributed.

Minimum competency testing in education

The criterion testing movement has, however, had one particular, very important effect: it has led to a much needed shift in emphasis from the properties of tests and towards the properties of items. By tackling the problem of defining criteria at the level of the individual item, the full complexity of item characteristics has been brought to light. One impetus for this process in both the UK and the USA has been a widespread concern for what has been perceived as a fall in school standards. Evidence to support these claims was given in the *Black Paper* in Britain, and in *A Nation at Risk* in the USA. The latter included the claim that, as a result of changed methods of schooling since the 1960s, 73 million Americans are functionally illiterate, that 13% of all 17 year olds in the USA are functionally illiterate, and that the College Board's Scholastic Aptitude Tests demonstrated a virtually unbroken decline from 1963 to 1980. Both of these publications led to widespread demands for some form of universal curriculum in the basic educational areas, largely in reading, writing and arithmetic, and to evaluate this universal curriculum there has been a demand for universal tests of these basic skills to monitor what is actually occurring in the schools.

A decline of basic standards, prima facie, seems to be a perfect situation in which to test the advantages of criterion referencing, for basic skills seem to be suitable for forming universally agreed criteria. If we take arithmetic as an example, we could say that every child must at a certain age at least be able to add up and multiply. This would be popular with many parents who feel it important for their children to know their times tables. But this on even superficial analysis turns out not to be simple at all. A child can be able to sing their times tables (rather like singing a French song) and not know about multiplication at all. Or they may be able to repeat that $6 \times 3 = 18$ but not know how to apply this; or they may know it for calculating purposes but not for enumerated objects and so on. These issues often turn on fine points of epistemology. The usual answer to this form of conceptual analysis is to make a call to popular consensus. It is argued that while many teachers and parents will have their own special views on what is important, they will generally be able in a series of meetings to produce a document which represents consensus. So long as such a consensus is available, then it should in principle be possible to devise appropriate tests. Once agreement has been reached on the appropriate curriculum for arithmetic and for the role of multiplication within it, then items to measure the achievement of these skills are possible.

In the 1980s the use of sophisticated criterion based techniques for assessing simple skills has increased, particularly in the USA, where Minimum Competency Tests have become mandatory in many states. These tests are designed to set minimum standards for schools and pupils in reading, writing, arithmetic and other learned skills. In a summary of survey findings in 31 states and 20 local districts, Berk (1986) summarizes the following common features of these programmes:

1. There is an emphasis on the acquisition of minimum skills or competence, usually academic skills (e.g., reading, math, writing) and/or life skills (e.g., following directions, filling out a job application, balancing a cheque book).
2. An explicit performance standard for pass-fail decisions is set, so that one can separate the competent from the incompetent.
3. The test results are used to make important decisions about individual students such as promotion to a higher grade (or retention at the same grade), awarding of a high-school diploma or a certificate of special recognition (or awarding a certificate of school attendance), or assignment to remedial classes.

However, the introduction of these testing programmes has not gone unchallenged, and many parents have taken the state education authorities to court on claims of unfair decisions based on test results. A series of cases has led to stringent attempts to demonstrate the reliability and validity of the tests used, and has also led to more openness in the definitions and establishment of criteria. Thus, for example, in the case of Debra P. v. Turlington (1983), the State of Florida carried out a large survey of instructional validity, and gathered a huge amount of evidence that the curriculum on which the tests were based was indeed taught in the classroom. This followed an earlier judgment that the state must demonstrate that the material on the test was actually taught in the classrooms to demonstrate content validity. A further development has been the widespread acceptance that there are no real objective standards available to define competences, and that the selection of the most important skills for the purpose of testing is highly subjective. This has not, however, led to a rejection of testing but to the development of political procedures and public strategies to obtain the consensus of all interested parties such that the definition of the curriculum and requirements for minimum competency can have credibility and meaning. Berk argues that the trend towards minimum competency testing will probably intensify in the 1990s.

Obtaining test scores by summing item scores

When a test is scored from its items it is usual to sum items. The main justification for this seems to be that it is normal practice as there is no a priori reason why a test should be scored in this way. When we do this we are effectively assuming that all of the items are equally important in their contribution to the test. This being so, it would seem sensible to review the actual importance of each item, and to use a score that is weighted for 'importance'. For example, if item 1 is considered of importance 1, item 2 of importance 2 and item 3 of importance 4, we could weight item 1 by 0.5, item 2 by 1, and item 3 by 2, thereby achieving a test score which more accurately represented the actual contribution of the items. In practice, however, this is rarely done, probably for pragmatic reasons. A common approach to scoring throughout psychometrics does have many practical advantages. In particular, it becomes easier to evaluate tests, to give instructions on scoring, and to set standards.

Although a common practice seems to have arisen in the manner in which item scores are combined to give a total test score, the interpretation of the relationship between item and total score has varied. From one point of view, items are seen as measuring sticks of varying length. Imagine measuring the length of a table by holding sticks of varying length against the table one after another. The length of the table will be given as the average length of the two sticks which were on either side of the actual table length, just shorter and just longer. Similarly, an individual's ability could be defined by the item which he or she just managed to pass and the item which he or she just failed. In practice, there would be some error in this approach, but we can see that the simple sum of items correct does give a fair estimate of test score. Another approach is to imagine a situation where all items have equivalent difficulty but where individuals with higher ability have a higher probability of getting each of these items right. Here again the simple summation of the number of correct responses gives an estimate of the individual's ability, which makes intuitive sense. Thus, whatever way we choose to think of the measuring process involved in the traditional item summation method, we achieve a match with the final score. It is this generality of the age-old technique which has given the traditional approaches to psychometrics so much staying power. Of course, all of these models assume that it makes sense to actually add the items, and, by implication, that the items are to some extent measuring the same construct.

The correction for guessing in objective knowledge based tests

One common concern with this traditional manner of looking at test scores has been that some subjects may artificially inflate their scores by guessing the answers. Thus, if we have a test composed of 100 statement type items to which each of the respondents has to agree or disagree, a rogue who knew nothing could obtain a score of about 50 by answering at random while an honest person who knew nothing would get zero from being unable to answer any question. One way of reducing this effect is to use multiple choice items rather than true/false; however, even here there can be a guessing artifact. If there are 5 alternative responses within the multiple choice questions then the rogue still has a 20% chance of getting the item right by guessing, giving a score of 20 on a 100 item test. A technique for tackling this problem is to apply a correction for guessing. There are several formulae for this in the literature but the following is most common:

$$C = (R - W) / (N - 1)$$

where C is the corrected score, R is the number of correct responses, W is the number of incorrect (wrong) responses, and N is the number of alternatives available. With true/false style items the number of alternatives is 2, so the formula reduces to 'number right' minus 'number wrong'. This formula has several interesting aspects. First, we can see that it is effective. The rogue who guessed all the items in the true/false test should on average get half right and half wrong, and the difference between these will be about zero, which seems appropriate. Second, we can fairly easily see the rationale for the formula: the 'number wrong' is effectively used as an estimate of the number of guesses, and when this number is estimated, the effect of the guessing can be eliminated. Thus in a true/false test, if a respondent has 8 incorrect answers, then it is assumed he or she obtained these by guessing. As there was a 50% chance of obtaining a wrong answer by guessing it is further assumed that the number of items guessed was 16, the expected number he or she would need to guess to obtain 8 wrong answers. Now the respondent has gained no advantage from the 8 wrong answers obtained by guessing, but has gained an extra 8 points for the 8 right answers, which are consequently deducted from his or her total score. A third aspect, however, leads to problems. What has effectively happened is that the respondent loses one scale point for each wrong item, that is, he or she is penalized for wrong answers. This information is often given in the test instructions when this type of correction is to be used, and there is no real penalization as the successful guesses effectively outweigh the unsuccessful ones. However, the formula assumes that a respondent either knows the answer to an item, or guesses. But in practice most guesses are inspired, and a person who guesses is more likely to be right than wrong. The formula therefore underestimates the amount of guessing and therefore undercompensates for it.

Let us now look at the effect of telling respondents that a guessing adjustment will be made. An honest person will take these instructions seriously and will avoid guessing, but the rogue who guesses, and who presumably makes some inspired guesses, will still achieve a higher score. The total effect of our formula, and our appeal to honesty, have thus had the net effect of giving an advantage to the rogue. Another difficulty with the use of guessing effects can be that they are viewed by respondents, particularly young children, as being unfair.

There is more to examinations than testing alone — they exist within a tradition which is an integral part of the social environment of personal advancement. Within this environment, success or failure are often attributed to luck or fate. What may seem like error of measurement to a psychometrician, e.g., where the answer to an item is known by a student because of some fluke, can be seen as a stroke of luck to a student. Thus, in a Latin unseen examination, if I know no Latin and yet appear to make a perfect translation from Latin to English because

I already knew the passage in English and am able to identify it from the recognition of a name or two in the Latin text, then first I am very lucky but second my score on the test is psychometrically invalid. However, there is a general belief that people to some extent deserve their luck and have to put up with fate, and this can also be applied to the guessing situation. Thus if a child guesses an item and gets the item right, this is not seen as an error which needs correction but a form of divine intervention. From such a perspective it seems churlish to remove it. This can be put another way. There are social conventions in the use of tests, and one of these is that the score on a test is the number of items a person has responded to correctly. This convention has a wide degree of acceptance, and it may be unwise to apply any form of transformation which undermines this acceptance, however apparently psychometrically justified.

For these and other reasons corrections for guessing are to be avoided in testing as much as is possible. It is much more effective simply to instruct subjects that if they do not know the answer they should guess. This way all get an equal chance. The only disadvantage is that now effective scale points do not start at zero. However, this zero has no true meaning in any case. A scale that runs from 50 to 100 is just as useful and valid. Unfortunately, there are some forms of test, particularly timed tests, where this is not applicable. With a timed test it is not expected that everyone would be able to complete the test in the time allowed, and consequently most respondents will have no opportunity to make guesses of the later items. Thus with these tests it may be necessary to apply a guessing correction. However, it is also an argument against the use of timed tests where it is avoidable.

Summary

There are several types of test and test item commonly used in psychometrics. Knowledge based tests and items can be distinguished from person based tests and items. The former measure the extent of a person's knowledge, while the latter measure personality, clinical symptoms, mood or attitude. Norm referenced items and tests are derived to see how a particular person's score compares with the population at large, while criterion referenced items and tests attempt to relate the respondent's answers directly to some outside criterion, usually the ability to carry out a task. Finally, items can be either entirely objective, where the scoring criteria can be completely specified beforehand, or open-ended as in essay tests or projective tests. For the latter it is impossible to eliminate the subjective element completely from the scoring process. All of these different types of item and test have their different uses, and which is to be preferred varies with the purpose to which the test is to be put.

Chapter four

Item analysis

In the stage of test construction following the construction of the test specification, we will be generating a large number of possible items. There is then the need to reduce these to a manageable number, and in doing so, to select the best. But how are we to make such a selection? The answer is provided by a procedure known as item analysis. Within the item analysis all the possible test items are subjected to a stringent series of evaluation procedures, individually and within the context of the whole test. This process takes place in two stages: first, a review by experts and second, a pilot study. In the first stage each item should be discussed with an expert, someone who knows and is familiar with the subject matter in question. The rationale for each item should be made explicit, and the stages of reasoning which the respondent may follow should be rehearsed. If the item is to be scored as right or wrong, then possible alternatives need to be explored, as it is occasionally the case that subjects may (correctly) be able to identify the distractors as correct under certain circumstances. The more care that is taken at this early stage the better, as once the test has been piloted we no longer have a completely free hand in making changes to the items, except by carrying out a re-pilot at further expense.

Item analysis statistics for knowledge based tests

For the pilot study a sample of subjects should be obtained with similar relevant characteristics to those people for whom the test is intended. The test is administered to these subjects, and an item analysis is then carried out on their responses. Classical item analysis in knowledge based tests has concentrated on two statistics, item facility and item discrimination.

Item facility

Item facility is obtained by calculating the ratio of the number of respondents who give the wrong response to the whole number of respondents. If all the subjects are wrong on an item, this statistic will be equal to 1; if nobody gets it wrong, the statistic will be 0. As the easier the item the higher the score, this statistic is generally called the item facility index (although, rather confusingly, the term 'difficulty value' is sometimes used).

The meaning of the facility index can be understood in two ways, a common-sense way and a statistical way. Looked at from a common-sense point of view we can ask, 'What would be the effect of leaving out an item of facility 0 from a test?' It can easily be seen that this would have no effect at all. As total test scores are calculated by adding up the number of items correct, an item which every subject gets wrong will not have made any contribution to any of the total scores. Hence the total scores would have been the same had the item never existed, and it is therefore redundant. The same argument can be applied to an item with facility 1, although here there is the apparent effect that the existence of the item has caused all subjects' scores to be increased by 1. In fact, this increase is more imaginary than real. If it is found that a child obtains a score of 0 on a geography test, this does not mean that the child knows no geography at all, but rather that the test was at too high a level for him. In fact, all normative statistics — variances, standard deviations, standard scores, etc., are not affected in any way when the same constant is added to all scores. In interval scale terms the addition of an item with facility value 1 to a test has no real effect.

Facility can be interpreted from a statistical viewpoint if it is viewed within the context of norm referenced testing. One presupposition of norm referencing is that the purpose of the test is to spread out individuals' scores along a continuum, and it follows from this that the larger this spread the better. A larger spread is equivalent to a greater test variance, and thus one way in which items can be judged for suitability for inclusion in the test is by examining whether or not they make a contribution to this variance. The variance of a group of respondents' scores on a test is made up of two components, one related to item variance and another related to the correlations between the items. Thus an item which has large correlations with other items in the test and which itself has a large item variance will be making a large contribution to the total variance of the test. An item which is uncorrelated with other items and which has a small item variance will be making a relatively low contribution. All items will probably be making some contribution of this sort, but if in item analysis we select only those items which make the larger contributions, then the overall test variance will be large, and the test will be improved.

An item variance is simply the calculated variance of a set of item scores, all ones and zeros if the test item is scored as right or wrong. The item variance of an item with facility 0 is zero, as all the subjects have responded in the same way; and the same is true if the facility is 1. More usually some of the subjects will get the item right and some will get it wrong, and in this case the variance is obtained by letting the facility index equal p, and calculating it from the general formula for obtaining item variance:

$$\text{Variance of item} = p \times (1 - p).$$

Thus, if half the people get the answer wrong, the facility index is 0.5 and the variance of the item is $0.5 \times (1 - 0.5) = 0.5 \times 0.5 = 0.25$. In fact this is the largest possible value for the variance of an item; the value gets smaller as p gets either greater or less than 0.5, and reaches 0 at the limit where $p = 0$ or 1. Whether we use a statistical formula or our intuition we arrive at the conclusion that items which some get right and some get wrong are giving us more information than those items for which all respondents tend to respond in the same way. Maximum information from an item is obtained when the number right is equal to the number wrong.

When the facility value is known for each item, this information can be used to select items for the final version of the test. Before this is done, however, it is best to calculate the other item analysis statistics, so that each item can be judged in its entirety on a whole range of different criteria.

Item discrimination

The second item characteristic of classical item analysis is slightly more complicated, but it can again be looked at from both a common-sense and from a statistical point of view. Consider the case of an item which turns out to be such that those people who obtain a high score on the test as a whole tend to get the item wrong, while those who obtain a low score on the test as a whole tend to get the item right. Here it would be suspected that something was amiss — in all probability the wrong answer had been specified as being correct. In any event it is clear that the item is not behaving as the item writer intended, and therefore is no longer conforming to the original test specification. Such an item is said to have negative discrimination. A more common occurrence is for an item to have zero discrimination — that is, the people with low scores on the test as a whole are just as likely to get that item right as those with high scores. We would tend to say that such an item was idiosyncratic. Whatever it was measuring was unrelated to whatever the test as a whole was measuring. Viewed from the statistical perspective, such an item also fares badly. If it is uncorrelated with the total test score, then it is almost certainly relatively uncorrelated with most of the other items in the test, and therefore is making no contribution to the variance of the test.

There are various ways of calculating the discrimination of an item. If we have the data on a computer, the easiest way is simply to calculate the Pearson product–moment correlation coefficient of the item scores with the test scores. This will tell us the extent to which each item correlates with the overall scale. This can be interpreted as the extent to which the item is actually making a contribution to the scale. Without a computer, the easiest approach is usually to find the mean score on the test for those people who get the item right and the mean score for those who get the item wrong, and find the difference between the two. While the figures yielded by this technique will not be absolute, depending on the number of items in the test, they will enable all of the items to be compared with one another in terms of their discriminability. If the difference is big and in the right direction the item is a good discriminator; if this difference is small, zero or negative, the item is a poor discriminator. There are many additional techniques for calculating discriminability, with different practitioners having their own special preferences.

Once the facility value and discrimination value are obtained for each item it is possible to begin to make a selection of good items and to eliminate the bad from the final version of the questionnaire. Items should be selected which have moderate facility, as this will ensure that the items chosen are ones which make a large contribution to the total score and that room in the questionnaire is not wasted by the inclusion of relatively uninformative items. As an additional bonus it is a good idea to balance the number of easy items against the number of difficult items, so that the average score on the test is about midway between the highest and lowest possible scores. This balanced set is more likely to show a normal distribution in subsequent use of the questionnaire which can be important as parametric statistics always assume that data are normally distributed. If the original test tended to be too easy (with most items having a facility greater than 0.5) or too difficult (with most items having a facility less than 0.5), this can be counteracted by selecting the same number of each, regardless of their original relative frequency. Similarly, all items with poor discrimination can be eliminated from the test by only choosing those items with the highest discrimination statistics for the final version of the test. This exercise, however, owes as much to common sense and convention as it does to statistics, and in particular there is a need to bear in mind the original test specification. Clearly if an entire column or row were eliminated from the blueprint, the test would be changed and it would lose content validity. Thus it is important to ensure that the general pattern of item distribution from the blueprint is retained, even if this involves accepting some relatively poor items from some cells at the expense of good items from others. To demonstrate the danger here, imagine a test which repeated the same item twenty times where this item had facility of 0.5. On statistical criteria alone all the items in this test would seem ideal, with the right facility and almost perfect discrimination. It is only when this result is compared with the distribution in the blueprint that the error can be seen — all the items are within the same cell, and thus the new version of the test does not reflect the test blueprint — there is no content validity.

Item analysis for person based tests

The procedure which has just been described for a knowledge based multiple choice test is generalizable, with slight modification, to the construction of almost all forms of test.

Item facility

While the term 'facility' might seem only to apply to knowledge based tests, where item responses are either right or wrong, the same approach can in fact be used for all forms of objective test. Thus, in a personality test for instance, if agreeing with a statement would give a person a higher score on the personality trait in question, the p value, the number who agree divided by the total number of respondents, gives an appropriate equivalent item analysis statistic. It is important to remember in these cases, however, that all items must be 'scored' in the same direction with respect to the trait. This is because, in personality tests, many of the items are reverse items. Thus in a schizotypal personality test the items 'I have no enemies' and 'Some people are out to get me' both measure paranoia, but in opposite directions. A high score on paranoia is thus represented by responding 'agree' to item 2, but 'disagree' to item 1. In practice it is often easiest when doing item analysis on these type of data to reverse all the 'reverse' items before the item analysis is carried out.

In a health questionnaire, for example, statements to which agreement indicates good health will be scored as 1 for 'agree' and 0 for 'disagree'. Statements for which agreement indicates bad health will be scored as 1 for 'disagree' and 0 for 'agree'. When the resultant scores are subjected to item analysis, the facility value will represent the extent to which the item is agreed with or disagreed with by the subjects in the pilot study, and again we would want to eliminate all items to which almost everyone agreed or everyone disagreed.

Within person based tests there tend to be situations in which there are more than two response options, not just right and wrong, or agree and disagree. Here again 'facility' values can still be obtained, but these will be the mean value across subjects of the item scores. Thus, if the possible responses are 'strongly agree', 'agree', 'undecided', 'disagree' and 'strongly disagree', these may be scored as 0, 1, 2, 3 and 4 respectively. Here extreme facility values are represented by 0 and 4 rather than by 0 and 1. This situation should not, however, be confused with the four or five possible responses in multiple choice knowledge based tests. Here one of the choices is right and the rest wrong, so that the item analysis still uses 0 and 1.

Item discrimination

The discrimination index for a person based test would represent the extent to which the item was measuring the same concept as all of the other items in the questionnaire. It will therefore again be calculated from the Pearson product–moment correlation coefficient between the item score and the total score, and will represent the extent to which the item is in fact measuring the trait in question.

Item analysis in criterion referenced testing

A claim which is often made in educational settings is that classical item analysis is designed for norm referenced tests, and therefore does not apply to criterion referenced settings (see Chapter 3). Although it is the case that the central idea behind the statistical rationale for classical item analysis is the paradigm for norm referencing, it does have relevance for criterion reference tests as well. Within criterion reference testing there remains the need to evaluate items to find out whether they are suitable for inclusion in the test. This means that all criterion referenced tests need to be piloted, and the evaluation of criterion referenced items still requires the examination of facility and discrimination as a first step. While a normal distribution of the eventual test scores is no longer necessary, it still remains useful for the items to be sufficiently challenging for the respondents, and therefore distributions are often found which, while not normal, are not extreme either. Berk (1984) recommends that item analysis in criterion reference testing should be based on an evaluation of the difference between facility values obtained before and after a programme of instruction. If a large difference is obtained, this can be taken as evidence that the item in question is valid as a measure of the skill taught. If the difference is small or zero, then the item may be invalid. To calculate this pre-instruction/post-instruction difference, item facility both before and after the period of instruction needs to be found; however, the difference itself is a measure of item discrimination rather than item facility. Berk goes on to look at item homogeneity (his name for item discrimination calculated by the correlation between item scores and total test scores) as a possible statistic for use in criterion related item analysis, and considers it is not of itself necessary in criterion reference testing. However, while it is true that it is not a priori necessary, it is usually the case that items in a test will be expected to relate to each other as part of our underlying conceptualization of what is being measured. If they fail to do so it may well cast doubt on whether we actually understand what we are doing. Berk places particular emphasis on the qualitative procedures of judgmental review of item objective congruence and content bias. These are both issues that benefit from increased emphasis, and apply to norm reference tests as well.

Psychological traits, true scores, and internal test structure

The consideration of item analysis so far has been based on the assumption that in some sense there is a construct which the test is measuring. Item discrimination in particular seems to make the added assumption that this construct is unitary or unidimensional. But suppose that there is no single underlying trait involved? What if, for example, in a geography test there is not one single underlying skill of achievement in geography, but that there are many independent skills such as map reading, memory, political understanding, and so on? This is a variety of the argument about the existence or otherwise of the true score within the theory of true scores previously considered in Chapter 2. It can further be argued that if the sub-components of a test are uncorrelated, then it makes no sense to add them up. It is only if we presume the existence of a true score on an underlying trait that it is possible to judge whether an item can 'contribute' to this trait. This latter point is a restatement of the rationale for eliminating items with zero discrimination, but it still leaves the question, 'To what extent are we justified in assuming a single trait to such an extent that items which fail to conform are eliminated?' It is at this point that differences appear in the item analysis process between the use of tests for selection and for assessment. If the eventual aim is selection, then we are obliged in the end to reduce our data to a binary statement — pass or fail. Within this constraint we are therefore bound to select data which are summative. We must be able to combine any elements into a single decision, and it therefore makes sense to choose items which conform to this procedure, that is items which are correlated with the trait in question as estimated by the test score. Where the test is to be used for assessment, on the other hand, we may in fact be interested in various attainments or traits within the data. While these will be evaluated as a totality, there is no special need for them to be additive as a whole, but only for each item to correlate with the particular set of items which are measuring the same aspect. Our major interest in the item analysis is to eliminate items which tell us little, and, within our requirements, to obtain the simplest possible interpretative structure for the remainder, perhaps within a profile of several sub-tests. In fact there is far more information available from the pilot study data than the statistics of classical item analysis, and one way in which this can be utilized is through factor analysis.

Item analysis for more complex situations

The use of factor analysis

Factor analysis is a procedure, originally developed by Spearman in the early part of the twentieth century but since refined by statisticians, which enables us to investigate the underlying structure of a correlation matrix. A correlation matrix is generated whenever the relationship between more than two variables is investigated, and its contents increase rapidly with each additional variable. In a 5 item test, for example, there are $5 + 4 + 3 + 2 + 1 = 15$ correlations, as each item correlates with each other item. When there are 10 items in the test the number of correlations is $10 + 9 + \ldots$, etc., which equals 55 correlations. A correlation matrix of all correlations between items in a 100 item test is very large indeed. Spearman was originally interested in the various correlations between intelligence sub-tests (verbal, arithmetical, spatial and so on), and developed the technique to find his common factor of general intelligence.

Factor analysis can be particulary useful in item analysis. Where there is indeed one underlying construct being measured this should emerge as a first factor. It is then possible, in principle, to select items which correlate with this first factor, which provides an alternative to obtaining the discrimination index. In fact, factor analysis can be more useful than this. Where no simple first factor emerges it can also show possible alternatives, and should be able to tell us how many factors actually are needed to describe the data. Unfortunately the approach is often unable to give unequivocal results. Unlike techniques such as analysis of variance, there is still always a strong subjective element in its interpretation. Further, it has been abused by attempts to extract too much meaning from particular data sets, and can also be vulnerable to breaches of its own statistical assumptions. In spite of these drawbacks factor analysis is beginning to regain its former popularity. Log-linear models have clarified issues surrounding its assumptions, and in circumstances where it is used as a tool, rather then a technique for proving hypotheses, it is invaluable.

One example of its use is in the identification of bias in the test, and in the selection of items which reduce this bias. A first factor will often be contaminated by acquiescence effects (the tendency of some people to always agree or disagree with everything), and a procedure called rotation can be carried out to find out what weightings (in this case functionally equivalent to item total correlations) would be obtained if this effect was eliminated. Other contaminating effects such as lying can be reduced by introducing 'lie' items into the pilot version of the test and rotating to a solution which eliminates these. Within tests designed for assessment it is often necessary to identify a number of sub-tests, and again factor analysis can indicate to us which types of sub-test should be used, and how these should be constructed. So long as factor analysis remains a tool, supplementary to but never overriding common sense, it continues to be one of the most useful statistical techniques available to test constructors. It is now available on computer, for example on SPSSX (Nie *et al*. 1983), so that we can expect its use (and unfortunately abuse) to grow.

Latent trait models and item response theory

Another technique of item analysis which has recently become popular is based on latent trait theory (Birnbaum 1968), and is more generally known as Item Response Theory (IRT). This provides an alternative approach to item selection from that provided by the classical method. It is far more precise than the classical model and thus has the potential of utilizing this precision to generate more accurate and sensitive ways of selecting items. The IRT approach is based on the concept of an Item Characteristic Curve (ICC), which, for each item, relates the probability of getting the answer right to the respondent's ability.

An example of an item characteristic curve is given in Figure 4.1. It can be seen that the ICC takes the form of a normal ogive, that is, a cumulative normal distribution. There should be nothing surprising about this as the ogive is just another version of the normal distribution, and is therefore to be expected where the effects of random error are included in observed measurements, as in all models based on the theory of true scores. Each item has its own curve, and it will be expected to move in an upward direction from left to right, although the extent to which it does this is a property of the item. The starting point on the left-hand side of the ICC frame represents the probability of a person with very low ability getting the item right. If the ability axis is started at a low enough level this might be expected to be always zero, but this only applies if there is no guessing effect. Thus if a person of very low ability guesses the answer to a multiple choice item with four choices he has a 25% chance of getting the right answer by chance and the curve for such an item would therefore be expected to begin at the 0.25 probability point of the y axis. If the ability axis is extended to a high enough level on the right-hand side of the ICC frame we might expect a probability of 100% that the response will be correct. However, even here this is not always the case. If the item is not in fact measuring what it is intended to measure, then even high ability respondents may not choose the item designated as correct, simply because from their point of view it is not so. There are other ways in which ICCs can vary. Some may be more or less flat while others may begin at a low level and follow

61

Figure 4.1 The Item Characteristic Curve (ICC)

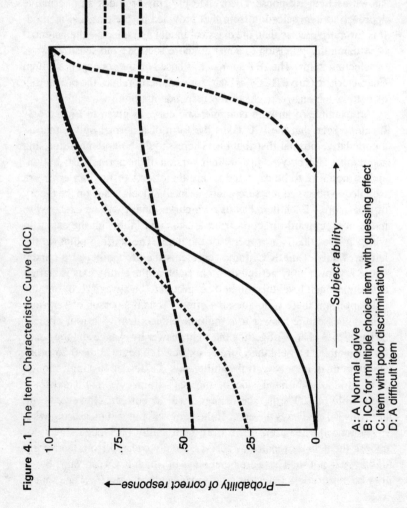

Probability of correct response

Subject ability

A: A Normal ogive
B: ICC for multiple choice item with guessing effect
C: Item with poor discrimination
D: A difficult item

A
B
C
D

1.0

.75

.50

.25

0

this path for a while, and then show a sudden increase and flatten out again at the top of the frame. This latter shape would be expected where an item has very high discrimination. Correspondingly, the flat items are those with low discrimination. Another form of variation is defined by a bunching effect to either the left- or the right-hand side of the frame. If the item crosses the 0.5 probability level well to the left, then it means that the item is easy. Subjects of moderate ability have a high probability of getting it right. If on the other hand the curve crosses the 0.5 probability point well to the right, then the curve must be for a rather difficult item.

The aim of item response theory is to look at the fundamental algebraic characteristics of these ICC curves and to try and model them in such a way that a set of equations can be extracted that can predict the curve from some basic data. This modelling is the same as that involved in the more familiar process of obtaining the equation to a straight line. This is, you will remember, based on the equation $y = a + bx$, so that if a and b are known then so is the position of the straight line itself within the xy frame. When the ICC ogive is modelled in this way the situation unfortunately turns out to be somewhat more difficult. However, now that faster and more powerful computers have been developed it is a real possibility. There is a general consensus that four variables are required to define an ICC. These are one subject variable (the subject's ability) and three item variables (which are called the item parameters). The three item parameters map on to the traditional notions of classical item analysis, i.e. one of them describes item facility, another item discrimination, and a third the guessing effect. If the values of the three parameters are known, then it is possible to reconstruct the item characteristic curve.

Unfortunately, the mathematical model of the full process is mathematically complex, time consuming and expensive in terms of computer usage. For these reasons attempts were made to simplify the full model by approximating the ICC with a lower number of parameters. The three basic models of item response which resulted have become known as the one, two and three parameter models, depending on how many of the three variables needed to describe the item characteristic curve (item facility, item discrimination, and the probability of getting the answer right with zero ability i.e. the guessing effect) are considered. The main proponent of the one parameter model has been Rasch (1980). The Rasch model became popular in the United Kingdom in the 1970s but has now fallen into disrepute as a result of its premature and rather ill-considered application on rather a wide scale. Rasch was able to show that if it is assumed that any guessing factor is held constant (as is the case if all items are of the same type), and if only items with equal discrimination are accepted, then some of the restrictions of classical psychometrics are loosened. In particular the model seemed to be able to generate, on computer, a single statistic for each item which enabled that item to be used in a wide variety of different situations, regardless of which other items were included in the test and of the particular subjects involved. This approach showed considerable promise in the calibration of item banks.

Item banks and the Rasch one parameter model

An item bank, in its widest definition, is merely a collection of items accumulated over time and stored, perhaps in a filing cabinet. Such a bank would be built up wherever there was a repeated need for testing in the same area — for example, the many multiple choice items used in the British medical examinations, or in the Hong Kong school selection system. Item banks are used to store items which can then be used for new tests. As expertise in item construction developed, with item constructors generating thousands of items over the years, a particular style of item began to stand out, and be used again. When an item bank contains far more items than will be actually required on any one occasion, there is the temptation simply to withdraw a few items at random each time testing is required. However, even with large banks it is still important to check the items, to pilot them, and to establish their reliability and validity. Within the classical model it is the test, rather than the bank, which is the basic unit. Clearly there is some redundancy in this approach. After all, each time an item is used considerable information is gathered about its properties, and this tends to be ignored if the item happens to be chosen again. Attempts have been made to retain the information on the facility and discrimination of each item, and to find some algorithm that would enable this information to be used later. The main difficulty was that each group of items was different, and it was here that the Rasch model began to look attractive. Rasch was able to show that, as long as all the items in the bank had equal discrimination, it was possible to produce a single item statistic (parameter) which was independent of the respondents used to pilot it, and of the other items included in the pilot. For this reason he called his technique both 'subject free' and 'item free'.

Let us consider how this would work. Assume we collect 1,000 items within a bank. To begin with none of the items would have a Rasch parameter. However, if we withdraw a set of 50 items at random from the bank and administer them to a group of respondents, each of these 50 will pick up some information towards its parameter. This will depend largely on its facility and will be tagged to the item within the bank. As further random groups of items are chosen then, so long as some of the pre-tagged items are included, the new items will also be tagged but with automatic adjustment made from any differences in the ability of the new group of respondents. This is possible as those items which were used in both the first and the second group provide information on this difference. As more items are tested in this way we should eventually have an item bank in which all items are tagged. As items are drawn on again and again, their tags become more certain, since new information is gathered each time. To score a set of Rasch scaled items from the bank, the subjects' responses and the item tags are fed into a computer program based on the Rasch algorithm, and a score is generated with respect to the bank as a whole, not just to the particular items administered. The score should be the same (within the usual margins of error) whichever items are chosen, and it should not matter whether the original tags were generated on a group of subjects whose ability was different.

This technique, if accurate, would be exceptionally useful to educational testers, particularly those dealing with very large populations. In the 1970s it proved particularly attractive in the United Kingdom to a group set up by the Department of Education and Science to monitor academic standards, which became known as the Assessment of Performance Unit (APU) (Gipps 1986). It seemed that if an item bank of appropriate items for measuring, say, mathematics achievement at age 11, was available, then by taking random sets of items from the bank for different groups of 11 year olds, it would be possible to compare schools, teaching methods and even, with the lapse of years between testing, the rise or fall of standards. However, this was not to be. It soon became apparent that there were several serious flaws within the model.

Problems with the Rasch model

First, it was noticed that a set of items identified as suitable for the finished test seemed to be more or less the same whether classical item analysis or the Rasch technique was used in selection. This generated a paradox. If the items in a classical test and in the Rasch scaled test were the same, how could it be that Rasch's claim that the test was item free and subject free was justified in the one case, but not in the other? The success of the Rasch model depended on selecting a special set of items, those with equal discrimination, while this was not a requisite of classical item analysis, which merely required good discrimination. In particular, an item which correlated very highly with the total test score should be accepted by the classical method and not by the Rasch method. It was particularly important for the claim of 'subject freeness' that the items should have the same discrimination as each other, as it was on this assumption that properties of the item for a group at one level of ability were extrapolated to a group at another level. If we find the two techniques accepting the same items, therefore, there is the implication that the test of equality of discrimination of the items is in fact not sufficiently powerful to eliminate items which are atypical in their discrimination. This indeed turns out to be the case. The test applied for parallelism within Rasch is a test of equivalent slope with acceptance based on proving the null hypothesis, a notoriously non-powerful statistic. If the test is not sufficiently powerful, then many of the items accepted into the bank will in fact not be parallel. If this is the case, then the claims of subject freeness and item freeness fail. If the technique were to be used, public policy on schools would be based on mistaken evidence.

A further difficulty for the technique arose from its being treated as if considerations of content validity were not necessary. It may have been felt that so long as a wide variety of item topics was used, taking a consensus of all the views of various educational theorists and practitioners, parents, politicians, religious leaders, etc., into consideration, then the item banks on a subject should be fairly representative. However, it turns out that comparisons between different groups of respondents are particularly sensitive to even small changes in consensus, and not in a fashion that can be ignored. Imagine, for example, that we wish to assess national standards in arithmetic at age 11, and to monitor the change in these over a ten year period. For the first testing session a consensus of views will be drawn up, and this presumably should relate to the agreed syllabus in arithmetic for children up to the age of 11 at that time. If we imagine 12 cells in the curriculum specification, then for good content validity the 12 cells in the test specification of the item bank will represent all of these. Items drawn at random from the bank will further be equally representative, showing no bias for or against particular cells of the blueprint. Random selections of items are administered to a random selection of 11 year olds, and ten years later a new random set of items is administered to a new random group of

11 year olds. It is at this later date that the problems become apparent. Consensus views are particularly unreliable over time (consider popular views on teaching mathematics over the last 10, 20, 30, 40 and 50 years), and the consensus view on arithmetic would almost certainly be different ten years on; and so, therefore, would be the arithmetic syllabus. New ideas will have been introduced, and old ideas dropped. The child taking the test at this later date will, however, be taking a test designed ten years earlier. The child will be asked questions based on some topics which are no longer taught, and will not be asked any questions about the new inclusions in the syllabus. Thus the more the curriculum changes, for better or worse, the more disadvantaged the child in the second testing session. Testing of this sort must always, therefore, suggest a falling of standards, and more so when improvements are made in the curriculum.

The future of item response theory models

It was for reasons of this type that the use of Rasch scaling techniques was discredited in British education. The use of some of the sub-tests on the British Ability Scale (Elliot, 1983) also seemed to be discredited as these similarly had depended on Rasch scaling techniques for their construction. However, the world-wide trend is towards an increase in the use of item response theory models, particularly in the USA under the lead of the Educational Testing Service in Princetown. Many psychometricians are coming increasingly to feel that reaction against the use of these models has been an over-reaction based on previous abuses, and on a premature exaggeration of their possibilities. One of the main drawbacks to these models in the 1970s was the complexity of the algorithms and their enormous use of computer power, which was too expensive and time-consuming for most applications. This was one of the reasons why the relatively simple one parameter model was preferred over the more complicated two and three parameter models. However, times have changed. Programs for carrying out analyses for the Rasch model are now available for personal computers (Bock and Mislevy, 1982), and even the three parameter model no longer presents the challenge that it once did (Hambleton and Swaminathan 1985). The technique has proved to be particularly useful within computerized testing, where the items to be presented can be adapted in difficulty on the basis of responses already given, enabling dependable results from administration of 50% fewer items (Haladyna and Roid 1983). The use of item response theory models for comparing the scores of respondents who have taken tests at different levels of difficulty (related to Rasch's claim of subject freeness) has additionally provided very useful. This might apply, for instance, when an easy and a more difficult version of the same examination system (such as within the GCSE in England and Wales) need to be combined to generate a common set of marks. The public need for this type of comparison, for example when an employer wishes to compare two applicants for a job with different types of qualification, cannot be ignored. As with many areas in selection, it is not so much a question of saying what ought to happen, as of ensuring that what does happen is done fairly and efficiently. It is important to point out that most of the criticisms of the Rasch model do not apply to the two and three parameter models. These make no assumptions about the equality of discriminability of the items, and the three parameter model additionally takes into account the effects of guessing.

Summary

There are several models which have been put forward to help in the selection of good items for a test. The basic paradigm, however, remains that set by classical psychometrics: the identification of facility levels and discrimination power within norm referenced knowledge based tests. This techique is easily modified for use in person based tests, or for application to criterion referenced testing situations. More recently, more sophisticated models have been proposed which take advantage of computer technology. These models are now beginning to come into their own. However, there is a need to use them with caution: they carry with them the same problems as those found with large statistical packages in statistics generally. It is important that those who use these more advanced techniques avoid being blinded by the computer, and retain a connection with the basic data. The impact of psychometrics on society is enormous, and those responsible must therefore know what they are doing. Responsibility cannot be abrogated to a computer.

Chapter five

Characteristics of tests

Within classical psychometrics, two of the most important aspects of a test are its reliability and its validity. Reliability has been defined as the extent to which the test is effectively measuring anything at all, and validity as the extent to which the test is measuring what it is purported to measure. If a test is unreliable it is impossible for it to be valid, so that it would be a logical impossibility to have a test which was valid but completely unreliable. On the other hand a test can be reliable but invalid.

Reliability

Reliability is often explained in terms of the measuring process in physics or engineering. When we measure, for example, the length of a table we assume that our measurements are reasonably reliable. We could check this out by taking several length measurements and comparing them. Even if we aim to be particularly precise it is unlikely that we will get exactly the same length each time. On one occasion the length of the table may be 1.989 metres, and on another 1.985 metres. But in most circumstances we would still be reasonably happy if the errors were only so small. In the social sciences on the other hand, unreliability of our measures can be a major problem. We may find that, for example, a pupil gets a score of 73 on a geography test on one occasion, and a score of 68 two weeks later on the same test, and we would probably feel that these figures were as close as we could reasonably expect in a classroom test. However, if the test in question was at university entrance, and the scoring system gave B for 70 and above, and C for below 70, and if the pupil was a university applicant who required B grades, we would certainly have cause for concern. It is because apparently reasonable levels of reliability for a test can have such devastating effects that we need first to make tests which are as reliable as possible, and second to take account of any unreliability in interpreting test results. All published tests are required to report details of reliability and of how it was calculated, and whenever a test is constructed and used, information on reliability must be included.

Test–retest reliability

There are several techniques for estimating the reliability of a test. The most straightforward is called test–retest reliability, and involves administering the test twice to the same group of respondents, with an interval between the two administrations of, say, one week. This would yield two measures for each person, the score on the first occasion and the score on the second occasion. A Pearson product–moment correlation coefficient calculated on these data would give us a reliability coefficient directly. If the correlation was 1, there would be perfect reliability, indicating that the respondents obtain exactly the same score on both occasions. This never happens (except perhaps by fluke) in psychological or educational settings. If the correlation between the two occasions is 0, then the test has no reliability at all: whatever score was obtained on the first occasion bears no relationship whatever to the score on the second occasion, and by implication, if the respondents were tested again, they would come up with another completely different set of scores. In these circumstances the scores are quite meaningless. If the correlation between the two occasions is negative, this implies that the higher the respondent's score the first time, the lower the second time (and vice versa). This never occurs except by accident, and if it does a reliability of 0 is assumed. Thus all tests can be expected to have a test–retest reliability between 0 and 1, but the higher the better. One advantage of using the correlation coefficient to calculate test–retest reliability is that it takes account of any differences in mean score between the first and second occasion. Thus if every respondent's score had increased by 5 points on the second occasion but was otherwise unchanged, the reliability would still be 1. It is only changes in the relative ordering or in the intervals between the scores which can affect the result.

Parallel forms reliability

Although the test–retest method is the most straightforward, there are many circumstances in which it is inappropriate. This is particularly true in knowledge based tests which involve some calculation in order to arrive at the answer. For these tests it is very likely that skills learned on the first administration will transfer to the second, so that tasks on the two occasions are not really equivalent. Differences in motivation and memory may also affect the results. A respondent's approach to a test is often completely different on a second administration (e.g. they might be bored, or less anxious). For these reasons an alternative technique for estimating reliability is the parallel forms method. Here we have not one version of the test but two versions linked in a systematic manner. For each cell in the test specification two alternative sets of items will have been generated, which are intended to measure the same construct but which are different (e.g., $2 + 7$ in the first version of an arithmetic test, and $3 + 6$ in the second). Two tests constructed in this way are said to be parallel. To obtain the parallel forms reliability, each person is given both versions of the test to complete, and we obtain the reliability by calculating the Pearson product–moment correlation coefficient between the scores for the two forms. Many consider the parallel forms to be the best form of reliability; however, there are pragmatic reasons why it is rarely used. When a test is constructed our main aim is to obtain the best possible items, and if we wish to develop parallel forms not only is there twice the amount of work, but there is also the possibility of obtaining a better test by taking the better items from each and combining them into a 'super test'. This is generally a more desirable outcome, and frequently where parallel forms have been generated in the initial life of a test, they have later been combined in this way, as for example in the later versions of the Stanford-Binet.

Split half reliability

A more widely used approximation to parallel forms reliability is split half reliability. For this technique a test is split in two to make two half-size versions of the test. If this is done in random fashion, a sort of pseudo-parallel forms is obtained where, although there are not necessarily parallel items within each cell of the test specification, there is no systematic bias in the way in which items from the two forms are distributed with respect to the specification. It is a common convention to take the two forms from the odd and even items of the questionnaire respectively, so long as this does indeed give a random spread with respect to the actual content of the items. For each individual two scores are obtained, one for each half of the test, and these are correlated with each other, again using the Pearson product–moment correlation coefficient. The resultant correlation itself is not a reliability. It is, if anything, the reliability of half of the test. This is of no immediate use as it is the whole test with which we have to deal. However, we can obtain the reliability of the whole test by applying the Spearman-Brown formula to this correlation:

$$r_{test} = (2 \times r_{half}) / (1 + r_{half}),$$

where r_{test} is the reliability of the test, and r_{half} is the correlation obtained between the two halves of the test. This tells us that the reliability is equal to twice the correlation between the two halves, divided by one plus this correlation. Thus if the two halves correlate 0.6 with each other, then:

reliability $= (2 \times 0.6) / (1 + 0.6) = 1.2 / 1.6 = 0.75.$

It is worth noting that the reliability is always larger than the correlation between the two halves. This illustrates the general rule that the longer the test the more reliable it is. This makes sense as the more questions we ask the more information we obtain, and it is for this reason that we will generally want our tests to be as long as possible, so long as there is time for administration and the respondents are co-operative. Of course, this only applies so long as the items are actually discriminating, that is, they are making a real contribution to the overall score (see Chapter 4 on item analysis).

Inter-rater reliability

All of these types of reliability relate in particular to objective tests, i.e. tests in which the scoring is completely objective. However, there are additional forms of reliability which are applicable where the degree of objectivity is reduced. For example, different markers of the same essay tend to give different marks, or different interviewers may make different ratings of the same interviewee within a structured interview. Reliability here can be found by correlating the two sets of marks or the two sets of ratings respectively using the Pearson product–moment correlation coefficient between the scores of the two raters. These forms of reliability are known as inter-marker or inter-rater reliability.

Interpreting the reliability coefficient

From the theory of true scores a very simple formula for relating error to reliability can be derived:

$$\text{Error variance} = \text{variance of test} \times (1 - r_{\text{test}}),$$

where r_{test} is the reliability of the test. The standard error of measurement is found as the square root of the error variance. Thus the error of measurement is equal to the standard deviation of the test, multiplied by the square root of one minus the reliability. If a test has a known reliability of 0.9, and a standard deviation of 15, then:

$$
\begin{aligned}
\text{the error of measurement} &= 15 \times \text{the square root of } (1 - 0.9) \\
&= 15 \times \text{the square root of } 0.1, \\
&= 15 \times 0.3, = 5 \text{ (approximately).}
\end{aligned}
$$

This is the standard deviation of error associated with any individual score on the test. From this we have some idea of the distribution of error about the observed score. This enables us to calculate a confidence interval for the observation. A confidence interval sets an upper and lower limit within which we can have a certain amount of confidence that the true score actually lies. Confidence intervals vary depending on the amount of certainty that is required. It may be important that certainty is high: we may want to risk being wrong only 1 time in 1000, and this would be called the 99.9% confidence interval. Or we may want just a rough and ready estimate such that the risk of being wrong was as high as 1 in 10 (the 90% confidence interval). The usual convention is to use the 95% confidence interval for most purposes, so that there is a 1 in 20 chance of being wrong. Although it is good to be accurate, the more accuracy that is required, the wider the confidence interval, and thus the greater the general uncertainty. For example, if a person had an observed score of 43 on a general knowledge test and we knew the standard error of measurement, we could obtain upper and lower limits for particular levels of confidence. The 95% level may give us the information that we can be 95% certain that the person's true score lies between 40 and 46, for example. If we need to be 99.9% certain we may have to say only that the true score lies between 35 and 50, perhaps too wide for useful application.

If it is assumed that the error of measurement is normal, then the statistical tables for the normal curve (z tables), which relate each z score to a particular probability, can be used to find the confidence interval. The appropriate z value for the 95% probability is 1.96 (a statistic worth remembering as it occurs in many different circumstances). The 95% limits themselves are thus obtained by multiplying the error of measurement by 1.96.

With an error of measurement of 5 (obtained from a reliability of 0.9 and a standard deviation of 15), an observed score of 90, and a 95% confidence interval, we can say that the true score lies between 90 plus or minus 5×1.95, that is, between about 80 and about 100. We could tell from this that another person with a score of 85 would not be significantly different, given the known amount of error which we have obtained from our knowledge of the test's reliability. This might be important if we needed to decide between these two people. In fact this example could easily have been obtained from scores on the Wechsler Intelligence Scale for Children (WISC), which does indeed have a reliability of about 0.9 and a standard deviaton of 15. We can see from this why so many psychologists are unhappy about using the WISC alone in making decisions about individual children.

One of the major uses of the reliability coefficient is in the evaluation of a test. Generally different types of test have different acceptable reliabilities. Thus individual IQ tests generally report reliabilities in excess of 0.9 and tend to average about 0.92. With personality tests reliabilities of greater than 0.7 are expected. Essay marking tends to produce notoriously low inter-rater reliabilities of about 0.6, even when complex agreed marking schemes are worked out in advance between the examiners. Creativity tests (e.g. 'How many uses can you think of for a brick?') are almost impossible to construct with reliability higher than 0.5. The lowest reliabilities are found in projective tests, such as the Rorschach ink blot test, where reliabilities of 0.2 and lower are not unusual. A test with such a low reliability is useless for psychometric purposes, but can be of use in clinical settings to provide a diagnostic framework.

When interpreting reliability coefficients, the spread of the scores of the sample under scrutiny must also be taken into account. This can only really be done by ensuring that the reliability has been calculated on a similar group to the one to which it is being applied. If a sample selected on some narrow criterion is used, such as university students, then reliability coefficients will be much smaller than for a whole population. Generally the larger the standard deviation of the group the higher the expected reliability. Thus, if the reliability from the whole population were to be combined with the standard deviation of the narrower group, the calculated standard error of measurement would be a considerable underestimate and might lead to serious mistakes.

Forms of reliability and forms of error

Decisions about the form of reliability to be used in judging a test cannot be made without a consideration of the nature of the error which is involved in each. There are two ways in which the reliability coefficient relates to error. First, there is a straightforward mathematical relationship between the coefficient itself and forms of error. Lord and Novick (1968) make an important distincion between error of measurement, error of estimation and error of prediction, and give different formulae for the calculation of each from the same reliability coefficient. The example above on the interpretation of IQ scores gives only the estimated error of measurement. Second, different circumstances will generate different reliability values for the same test depending on differences in the source of the error. If a test is administered with a one week interval between two administrations, then the error is composed of random elements which may have increased or decreased the respondent's scores on the two occasions — lack of sleep, hunger, illness, revising the right or the wrong material, and so on. If the test is given in split half mode, but at one sitting, the form of error is different. It is now error due to the different manner in which the two forms are sampled from the same domain. With inter-rater reliability the error is due to the different strategies and values of the raters, and is independent of the actual peformance of the respondents. Which of these errors is appropriate and which reliability is correct? Thorndike (1947) defined five different forms of variance which would be found operating within a reliability coefficient:

1 Lasting and general: e.g., general test taking ability.
2 Lasting but specific: e.g., knowledge or ignorance regarding a particular item that appears in one test form.
3 Temporary but general: e.g., buoyancy or fatigue reflected in performance on every test given at a particular time.
4 Temporary and specific: e.g., a mental set that affects success in dealing with a particular set of items.

5 Other, particularly chance success in 'guessing'.

All these sources of error can be operating at the same time, so it is to be expected that reliability coefficients will differ in different circumstances and on different groupings and samplings of subjects. Can these influences be disentangled? The answer is a qualified yes, the qualification being that to do so in practice can be a complicated matter.

Generalizability theory

Cronbach and his colleagues have carried out a thorough investigation of the analysis of different forms of error. Their approach has become known as generalizability theory (Cronbach et al. 1972). In this they use an analysis of variance model to relate the various reliability and validity test evaluation statistics directly to test application. Within multivariate analysis of variance and covariance models in particular, conceptions of the nature of error have changed considerably since the early days of the theory of true scores. This framework makes an immediate and clear distinction between, for example, the error term as estimated between a group of subjects and the within subject error term which is obtained when repeated measures are taken on a single subject. Empirical evidence as well as theory have now shown that these sources of error often show large quantitative differences. Similarly, error terms between groups may be different from those between subjects, and further estimated differences are found depending on whether the variation between groups is fixed or random. For a more detailed consideration of error terms in analysis of variance see Winer (1962). Cronbach and his colleagues were able to show that the classical techniques within the design, construction and application of psychometric tests could be treated as multi-level models within analysis of variance. As the mathematics of this latter area is very well developed, they were thus able to make its increased conceptual clarity and practical precision available to psychometrics. They further argue that the distinction between reliability and validity is a false one, being a matter of degree which can only have meaning in terms of how the tester intends to generalize from the test results. They further argue that it is only through this generalization that test scores can have any meaning whatsoever.

One particular innovation of the generalizability model is its full statistical underpinning of the functionalist approach. The test construction process is integrated within the same 'experimental' setting as the test application. Thus as well as identifying particular sources of error within the construction phase, the need for each such source is extrapolated backwards from the use to which the test is to be put. Cronbach identifies four different kinds of decision which may need to be made within this applied setting, and points out that the appropriate reliability and error term is different for each:

1 An absolute decision about whether an individual's score exceeds a predetermined cut-off point. This is assumed to be a generally criterion referenced comparison.
2 Comparison between two courses of action for an individual. This type of decision is particularly common in guidance where the person may choose one curriculum rather than another.
3 Comparisons between persons or groups.
4 Conclusions about the relationship between a pair of variables, e.g. between creativity and the schizotypal personality.

The general advice given in Cronbach's book is exceptionally sound, but unfortunately the practical application of the approach has not been widespread. This is probably due to its complexity. To devise such models is difficult, time consuming and expensive. Further, its extreme functionalism, which argues against the use of the same test in changed circumstances without serious revalidation, means that the full implementation of the generalizability approach is out of the reach of most practitioners who work in situations where resources are limited.

Cautions in the use of reliability coefficients

The interpretation of a reliability coefficient is no simple matter. Although most researchers would not wish to become involved in the complexity of the models generated by Cronbach's generalizability theory, a high degree of awareness of possible sources of bias is required. All published tests are required to report data on reliability, and this needs to be properly interpreted in terms of the samples used and the types of reliability coefficients obtained, as well as in terms of the intended use of the test. It would be inappropriate, for example, in the use of a test for an experiment with university students, to quote the reliability coefficient for the test on the population as a whole. The most important element in the use of reliability coefficients is human judgment.

Validity

The validity of a test also has many different forms. There are several categorization systems used, but the major groupings include face validity, content validity, predictive validity, concurrent validity and construct validity.

Face validity

Face validity concerns the acceptability of the test items, to both test user and subject, for the operation being carried out. This should never be treated as trivial. If respondents fail to take the test seriously the results may be meaningless. For example, some adults with cognitive impairment may be expected to have the same overall score on intelligence tests as 8-year-old children, but they may well object to the use of childish material in a test designed for them. Evaluation of the suitability of a test must include consideration of the style and appropriateness of the items for the purpose in hand, in addition to any more formal test characteristics.

Content validity

The content validity of a test examines the extent to which the test specification under which the test was constructed reflects the particular purpose for which the test is being developed. In an educational setting, content validation will generally involve a comparison between the curriculum design and the test design. In the use of a selective test for employment, the content validity will be the extent to which the job specification matches the test specification. Content validity is thus the principle form of validity for the functional approach to psychometrics, and has sometimes been described as criterion related validity in circumstances where the test designer is using the criterion referenced framework for skills learning and curriculum evaluation. Content validity is fundamental to psychometrics and is the main basis by which any test construction programme is judged. Content validity has to be judged qualitatively more often than quantitatively, as the form of any deviation from validity is usually more important than the degree. Essentially, if the test specification is not reflecting the task specification, it must be reflecting something else, and all else is a potential source of bias.

Predictive validity

Predictive validity is the major form of statistical validity, and is used wherever tests are used to make predictions. For example, the use of a test for job selection or for a programme of instruction where the test is intended to predict eventual success in these areas. Predictive validity is represented as a correlation between the test score itself, and a score of the degree of success in the selected field, usually called 'success on the criterion'. Thus, for example, in the use in England and Wales of GCE A level grades to select candidates for university, it might reasonably be assumed that the number and grade of A levels is related to degree of success at university. We could generate scores on the test by combining A level grades in some way (e.g., for each person, grade A = 6, grade B = 5, grade C = 4, etc., the scores for all examinations being summed). Similarly a score of success at university could be generated by assigning 0 to a fail, 1 to a pass degree, 2 to an third-class degree, etc., with a first-class degree having the highest score. A simple Pearson product–moment correlation coefficient between A level scores and degree-class scores would give a measure of the predictive validity of the A level selection system. If the correlation was high, say, over 0.5, we might feel justified in selecting in this way, but if it turned out to be zero we would certainly have misgivings. This would mean that students' success at university had nothing to do with A level scores, so that many people with one E grade, for example, could have had as good a chance of getting a first-class degree as those with three A grades. The A level selection procedure would then have no validity.

One common problem with predictive validity is that individuals who are not selected do not go on to produce a score on the criterion (people who do not go to university have no scorable degree class), so that the data are always incomplete. It is normal practice to use the data available, and then justify extrapolation downward. Thus if individuals selected with three C grades do worse than individuals selected with 3 B grades, it would be extrapolated that those with 3 Ds would have fared even less well. However, there must always be some uncertainty here.

Concurrent validity

Concurrent validity is also statistical in conception and describes the correlation of a new test with existing tests which purport to measure the same construct. Thus a new intelligence test ought to correlate with existing intelligence tests. This is a rather weak criterion on its own as the old and new tests may well both correlate and yet neither be measuring intelligence. Indeed this has been one of the major criticisms directed against validation procedures for intelligence tests, particularly when the conceptualization of intelligence in the later test is derivative of the conceptualization in the first, thus producing a 'boot strap' effect. However, concurrent validity although never sufficient on its own is important. If old and new tests of the same construct fail to correlate with each other then something must be seriously wrong.

Construct validity

Construct validity is the primary form of validation underlying the trait related approach to psychometrics. The entity which the test is measuring is normally not measurable directly, and we are really only able to evaluate its usefulness by looking at the relationship between the test and the various phenomena which the theory predicts. A good demonstration of construct validation is provided by Eysenck's validation of the Eysenck Personality Inventory, which measures extraversion/introversion and neuroticism. It was not possible for Eysenck to validate this scale by correlating respondents' scores on the extraversion scale with their actual amount of extraversion. After all, if this was known there would be no need for the scale. However, he was able to suggest many ways in which extraverts might be expected to differ from introverts in their behaviour. On the basis of his theory that extraverts had a less aroused central nervous system he postulated that they should be less easy to condition, and this led to a series of experiments on individual differences in conditionability. It was shown that, for example, in an eye blink conditioning experiment with a tone heard through headphones as the conditioned stimulus and a puff of air to the eye as the unconditioned, extraverts developed the conditioned eye blink response to the tone on its own more slowly than did introverts. He suggested that extraverts should also be less tolerant of sensory deprivation, and that the balance between excitation and inhibition in the brain would be different between extraverts and introverts, which led to a series of experiments. He also suggested that the EEG would vary, with extraverts showing a less aroused EEG, and this again could be tested. And finally he was able to point to some simulations of extravert and introvert behaviour, for example the effect of alcohol which produces extraverted behaviour. The validation of the construct of extraversion consists of a whole matrix of interrelated experiments. From this Eysenck concluded that extraverts condition more slowly, are less tolerant to sensory deprivation, are less sensitive to inhibiting drugs and are generally different from introverts on a whole variety of other psychophysiological and psychophysical tests. He claimed that his theory that extraversion had a biological basis was supported as it was able to provide a unified explanation for all these findings. Construct validation is never complete, but is cumulative over the number of studies available, and has many similarities to Popper's (1972) idea of verification in science. It is thus a reflection of a particular view of the scientific process, and is integrated within the positivist and hypothetico-deductive view of science.

Standardization

Once a test has been constructed it needs to be standardized. Standardization has two elements: first the need to obtain information on the test scores of the general population by taking appropriate samples, and second the need to obtain a set of principles by which raw data from the test can be transformed to give a set of data which has a normal distribution. This latter becomes particularly important if the scores need to be subjected to statistical analysis, as is usually the case. All parametric statistical tests, factor analysis, and most of the advanced techniques available make the initial assumption that data are normally distributed.

If the only information that is available following the administration of a test is one respondent's score, then it will tell us nothing about that person. For example, suppose we are told that Bertrand scores 23 on an extraversion test. Is this high, or low? Before we can make an interpretation we need to know what a score of 23 represents. This may be from norm referenced information, given by knowledge of the general population mean and standard deviation for extraversion scores. With this extra information we can say how extraverted Bertrand is in comparison with everyone else. Or it may be criterion related — for example, there may be information from the test handbook to tell us that people with extraversion scores of 22 and higher like going out all the time, or have difficulty settling down to a quiet read.

Comparison or criterion information of this type must be made available when a test is published. Norm referencing procedures are much more common than criterion referencing, largely because they are easier to carry out, and because for many tests it is extremely difficult to give clear and specific criteria. In order to obtain comparison data for a norm referenced test, a population must be specified which is directly comparable to the population of intended use. Thus, a test of potential to do well in business, used to select persons for admission to business school, must be standardized on business school applicants. If the potential sample is large, then the information can be obtained by a process of random or stratified random sampling. For information on the whole population of adults in a country, a random sample might be taken from the electoral register. Comparison data may be presented in raw form, as for example in the Eysenck Personality Inventory, where we are able to read in the handbook that the average extraversion score is about 12, with a standard deviation of about 4. We can tell from this that a person with an extraversion score of 22 is two and a half standard deviations above the mean. As extraversion scores on the population are known to be approximately normally distributed, we can find from tables of the normal curve (z tables), that less than 1% of the population has a score this high. The normal population data may sometimes be given separately for different groups, and this often enables a more precise interpretation. The extraversion norms, for example, are given for men and women separately, for different ages, and for different occupational groups. This information is important where comparisons are to be made within a group, rather than with the population as a whole. A situation where this might be useful could be in assessing mathematics ability among applicants for university places on mathematics courses. Here we would be interested in how applicants compared with each other, and the fact that they all performed in the top 50% of ability in mathematics in the population at large would be relatively uninformative.

Standardization to z scores

The interpretation of scores in terms of percentages within the general population is easy to understand, and it maps very well on to the pattern of the normal curve. Thus, from z tables, which are available in nearly all statistical textbooks, we know that a person who is above average is in the top 50%, a person who is one standard deviation above the mean is in the top 16%, a person who is less than 2 standard deviations below the mean is in the bottom 2%, and so on. For this reason, the comparison of an individual's score with the norm is often given in terms of the number of standard deviations with which it differs from the mean. In the earlier example of Bertrand with an extraversion score of 22, it was clear that with a mean of 12 and a standard deviation of 4, his score is 2.5 standard deviations above the mean. This score of 2.5 is referred to as the standard score, and is given more formally by the formula z = (score − mean score) / (standard deviation); in this case $z = (22 − 12) / 4 = 2.5$. The process of determining the population data, and using this to provide a method for transforming raw scores to standard scores is called test standardization. This is normally carried out either by providing data on the mean and standard deviation of the test together with a formula, or by providing a transformation table or graph.

Standardization to T *scores*

Transformed z scores on a test normally range between − 3.0 and + 3.0, and have a mean of zero. This is not a very convenient way to present an individual's score; school children in particular might tend to object if told that their score on a test was − 1.3! There is, therefore, a set of conventions which are applied to these standard scores to make them more presentable. The most common of these are the T-score, the stanine and the 'IQ' format. For T scores we multiply the z score by 10 and add 50. Thus a standard score of − 1.3 becomes $(− 1.3 \times 10) + 50$ = 37; much more respectable. The advantage of this format is that it turns the scores into something which resembles the traditional classroom mark, which normally has a mean of about 50 with most scores lying between 20 and 80. Unlike most classroom marks, however, it is very informative. If told that someone had scored 70 on a classroom mathematics test, we would not have any information unless we knew the marking scheme — it might be that a particular teacher always gives high marks. However, if the scores had been transformed to T scores, then because we already know that T scores have a mean of 50 and a standard deviation of 10, it is immediately clear that a score of 70 is two standard deviations above the mean. This is equivalent to a z score of 2, and by working backwards through the z tables we can easily find that such a score is in the top 2% of scores on that test.

Standardization to stanine scores

The stanine technique transforms the standard scores to a scale running from 1 to 9, with a mean of 5 and a standard deviation of 2. This standardization is widely used, as a set of scores from 1 to 9 (rather like marking out of 10) has much intuitive appeal. There are no negatives and no decimals which are, by convention, rounded off either downwards or to the nearest whole number. The advantage of the stanine over the T

score is that it is sufficiently imprecise not to be misleading. Most tests have only a limited precision. A T score of 43, for example, would be equivalent to a stanine score of 4, as would a T score of 41. The difference between 41 and 43 is much too small to be of any real significance but their bold statement within the T format does give a misleading impression of precision.

Standardization to IQ format scores

The 'IQ' format originated when the definition of Stanford-Binet IQ scores was changed from one based on the ratio of mental age to chronological age (the original meaning of 'Intelligence Quotient'), to the now widely used standardization approach. The IQ transformation is based on a mean of 100 and a standard deviation of 15; thus a standard score of -1.3 becomes an IQ score of $(-1.3 \times 15) + 100 = 80.5$ (or 80 when rounded off). An IQ score of 130 (that is $100 + (2 \times 15)$) is two standard deviations above the mean and, as two standard deviations means a z of 2, we can tell from z tables that such a score or higher would be obtained by less than 2% of the population. Some IQ tests use different standard deviations — for example, Cattell uses 16 scale points rather than 15. IQ style scores are best avoided by psychometricians today. They have become something of a cult, and their extrapolations bear very little relation to normal scientific processes. IQs of 160, for example, often appear as news items in the media, yet 160 would be 4 standard deviations above the mean. As such a high score would occur in the general population only 3 times in 100,000, we would need to have had a normal group of about 1,000,000 individuals to obtain the relevant comparisons. Usually tests are standardized on less than 1,000. Even the WISC, with its standardization group of 20,000, had relatively few subjects at each comparison age. The behaviour of individuals at probability levels of less than 3 in 100,000 is not something which can meaningfully be summarized in an IQ score. The whole conception of a unitary trait of intelligence breaks down at these extremes.

Normalization

All of these standardization techniques (the z score, the T score, the stanine, and the 'IQ' format) make the assumption that scores for the general population already have a normal distribution. There are often good reasons why a normal distribution might be expected, and it is common practice to carry out item analysis in such a way that only items which contribute to normality are selected. This can be done by selecting only the appropriate items within the item analysis (see Chapter 4). However, there are occasions when sets of test scores have different distributions (perhaps with positive or negative skew, or having more than one mode) and here alternative techniques for standardization are required. Statistical techniques are available to test for the existence or otherwise of normality. Perhaps the most straightforward of these is to split the data up into equal interval categories (say, about 5) and to compare (using the chi-square test of goodness of fit) the actual number of scores in each with the number which would be expected if the data had a normal distribution. Tests of normality are not particularly powerful, however, so that if there is doubt it is best to attempt to normalize the data in one of the following ways.

Algebraic normalization

The easiest technique for normalization is algebraic transformation. If the distribution of scores is positively skewed, for example, with most of the scores being at the lower end of the scale, then taking the square root of each score will produce a more normal distribution. The square rooting process has a stronger effect on the large, more extreme, figures. With extreme positive skew, log transformations can alternatively be used. All of these techniques are particularly important if the data are to be analysed statistically, as most statistical tests assume a normal distribution. Once an appropriate transformation has been found, it is usual to present the results in a table so that any test user can read off the transformed scores directly, rather than have to carry out a complicated algebraic operation (see Table 5.1).

Table 5.1 Transforming raw scores to stanine scores

Raw Score	Standardized Score
16 or less	1
17 to 21	2
22 to 25	3
26 to 29	4
30 to 33	5
34 to 37	6
38 to 41	7
42 to 46	8
46 or more	9

From the Golombok Rust Inventory of Marital State (GRIMS).

It has been argued that this transformation procedure is unnatural, and does not do full credit to the true nature of the data. However, this view is based on a misunderstanding. For norm referenced tests, the data really only have a true nature in relation to the scores of other individuals, while even in criterion referenced tests the data are rarely at the interval level of measurement, the minimum level required for distribution effects to have much meaning. Further, the data only have functional meaning in relation to the tasks to which they are put (e.g. t tests, correlations, etc.), and these generally require normally distributed data.

Graphical normalization

For some data samples (particularly where there is more than one mode), the deviations from normality of the raw population scores are too complicated to be eliminated by a straightforward algebraic transformation, but these situations can generally be dealt with by the construction of a standardization transformation graph, which makes a percentile to normal transformation.

For a standardization transformation graph (see Figure 5.1), the data are first arranged in order of size, and then cumulative percentages are found for each point on the rank. Thus, for a sample with 100 subjects, and in which the top two subjects score 93 and 87 respectively, we mark 99% at 93 and 98% at 87, and so on. With different sample sizes it will not be quite so straightforward, but the appropriate scaling can still achieve the desired results. We then plot the raw score (x axis) against the percentile score (y axis). This may well be a rather messy curve, but we can use our judgment to smooth it out, particularly in the areas where discrepancies seem to be due to few subjects. We can then use the known relationship between the z score and the percentile from the z tables to give us standard score equivalents for each raw score; $z = 0$ is equivalent to the 50% cumulative percentile, $z = 1$ to the 84% cumulative percentile, $z = -1$ to the 16% cumulative percentile, and so on. The recommended transformations will appear either as a transformation graph, with the percentile score axis stated as standard equivalents, or in transformation tables.

Summary

Once a test has been constructed it is necessary to be able to describe some of its general properties and to present the test in a form in which

Figure 5.1 Graphical normalization.

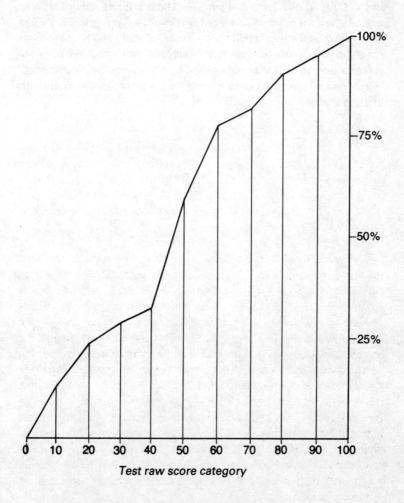

The graph is constructed from data by noting the percentage of respondents with raw scores of 10 or less, 20 or less and so on. Standardized scores can be obtained by reading the percentile associated with a particular raw score and translating this with Z tables. Alternatively, the Z values may be added to the Y axis as scale points.

it can be easily used. The reliability of the test must be found, and quoted in a clear and precise form such that future users are able to obtain some idea of the amount of error which might be associated with the use of the test for their own particular purpose. Data on the validity of the test must be given for as broad a range of applications as possible. Data must be provided on the population norms, both generally and for particular sub-groups which may be of interest. Finally, information should be given on the manner in which the data should be normalized and transformed to a common format to enable comparisons between the results of different studies.

Chapter six

Bias in testing and assessment

It is important that all tests be fair and be seen to be fair in their use. However, fairness only makes sense when viewed within a wider social and psychological perspective. Taken from an individual perspective, unfairness occurs when a wrong decision is made about an individual on the basis of a test result. Yet wrong decisions are made all the time, particularly when an individual's score is near the cut-off. If, for example, a student needs a B grade to gain entrance to a degree course, and the examiners have decreed that a B is equivalent to 80% on the test, and the student has obtained 79%, then there must be a statistical chance of at least 1 in 3 that a mistake has been made. Now from the point of view of the examiners who will be looking at the overall perspective, the best that can be hoped for is that mistakes will be kept to a minimum. Given the limited number of places available, and the lack of definitive knowledge of what makes for success in a course, it would be unrealistic to hope for any high degree of accuracy near the cut-off point. Yet it is unlikely that the unsuccessful student will find this argument acceptable. A consideration of this issue rapidly shows us that there exist a series of social conventions within society concerning what is considered as fair and unfair in these circumstances, and these conventions are informative as they often do not agree with conceptions of bias as viewed from the point of view of the statistician.

Bias and fairness

Consider for example a situation where half of the students taking an examination go, of their own volition, to a rather lively party the night before. Suppose all of these students scored on average five points less on the examination than all other candidates. In these circumstances it could be argued from a statistical point of view that the scores of the party-goers would be subject to statistical bias, and it would be reasonably easy to adjust for this bias — say by adding five points to the score of any person who was at the party. Now it is clear that this procedure, which may give a statistically better estimate of the true score, would be extremely unlikely to be accepted by the examinees or by society as a whole, and would probably even make the party-goers feel a little uncomfortable.

There is a general set of conventions about what examinees will accept as fair. If an examinee revises a set of possible examination questions which, although plausible, do not in fact occur in the examination, then a low mark will tend to be put down to bad luck rather than unfairness, even though a case for the latter could certainly be made. The ideology of these conventions is complex, as has been found by examination boards who attempted to make allowance for dyslexia. Generally the conventions allow exceptions for dyslexia so long as it is a medical condition, but do not make allowance for poor spelling, even though this is one of the major diagnostic criteria of dyslexia! A similar problem is found by school teachers who attempt to introduce a correction for guessing into their marking (see Chapter 3). In a true–false knowledge test, pupils who guess have a 50% chance of getting the right answer, so that if there are, say, 100 items then a pupil who knows nothing but guesses will have an expected score of 50. However, if the number of wrong responses is used as an estimate of guessing, then the score can be corrected. Children, however, do not take kindly to this procedure. From their perspective, if an item is guessed and the right answer is achieved, there is an entitlement to the mark obtained.

People will accept a certain amount of ill-luck within testing procedures so long as it conforms to pre-existing social conventions, and this is not generally seen as unfairness. The major cases of perceived unfairness at the individual level are where items have been included in the testing procedure which are not relevant to the selection or assessment process involved. Thus, for example, it is seen as unfair if a bank excludes short people for service as tellers. Issues of relevance, however, nearly always involve issues of group membership, and thus issues of bias. Bias in a test exists if the testing procedure is unfair to a group of individuals who can be defined in some way. The major issues of test bias involve race, linguistic minorities, sex and cultural differences, although other categorizations are important in particular circumstances (e.g., social class, height, age, sexual orientation, physical attractiveness, etc.).

Forms of bias

It is crucial that tests used for selection should be free from racial bias, and indeed it is illegal in many countries to select individuals on the basis of racial membership. With the advent of equal opportunities legislation in the USA, the UK and other countries in the 1970s, many of the old tests were unable to meet the stringent requirements for fairness required by the courts. Indeed many intelligence tests, and the Wechsler Intelligence Scale for Children (WISC) in particular, have been outlawed in many states within the USA. Test development since then has been far more systematic in its attempts to eliminate bias. There are three major categories of test bias: item bias, intrinsic test bias and extrinsic test bias.

Item bias

Item bias is the most straightforward in so far as it is fairly easy to iden-tify and therefore to rectify. This describes a situation where the bias exists within the individual items of which the test is composed. For example, items developed in the USA which ask about money in terms of dollars and cents would not be appropriate for use in England. Linguistic forms of item bias are the most common, especially where idiomatic usages of language, such as the use of the double negative in standard English, are not allowed. This is a particular difficulty with a diverse and widely used language such as English. If a person learns international scientific English, rather than idiomatic English, they may well be perfectly fluent within a work situation but still be disadvantaged by items generated by users of English as a first language. Similarly, particular dialects which use different grammatical structures in, for ex-ample, the use of the double negative may again be vehicles for bias. This effect has been found in a comparison of the responses of black and white children in the USA to Metropolitan Reading Test items which incorporate the double negative (Scheuneman 1975). Of the 55 items tested, 10 involved some negative structure, for example 'mark the picture which shows neither a cat nor a dog'. Of the 7 items which were found to be biased, 6 were of the negative form. Scheuneman also discovered item bias against non-oriental children in the Otis-Lennon School Ability Test (OSLAT) for visual matching and embedded figures tasks involving letters, numbers, letter-like forms and artificial letters. 8 out of 26 such items of which 5 involved hidden letters, were found to be biased in this way. It was hypothesized that oriental children were more familiar with the use of ideographic written forms in their alphabet. Items of all of these types have often been included in IQ tests.

Identifying item bias

While item bias is simple to identify and eliminate in principle, it is unfortunately not checked as often as it should be. The easiest way to check is to carry out an item analysis separately for the groups involved. First an appropriate group sub-structure must be identified, for example men versus women, or speakers of English as a first versus second language. Once this has been done the facility values of each item in the item analysis are compared between the groups. This can easily be done if the items are placed in order of facility for one of the groups, so that the deviations can be recognized in the other. Let us suppose that items a, b, c, and d have facilities of 0.85, 0.76, 0.68 and 0.63 respectively in group 1, while for group 2 the facilities for these items are 0.87, 0.45, 0.63 and 0.61. We can easily see that item b is idiosyncratic, and once it has been identified it can be deleted or changed. While it is unlikely that the items will have exactly the same facility for the two groups, we have a rough idea of what to expect and a simple inspection will often suffice.

If deemed necessary, it is also possible to carry out statistical tests for the existence of item bias. There are many ways in which this can be done, but the most straightforward is probably a two-way (group by item) analysis of variance with the facility value as the dependent variable. The almost certainly significant main effect for items is not of any real interest, while any statistically significant difference between groups will represent other forms of bias than item bias. However, the group by item interaction will give a straightforward test of item bias, which can be repeated as the offending items are identified and eliminated.

Cleary and Hilton (1968) have pointed out that there is some error in this approach as facility value calculations are based on binary data (0 for fail and 1 for pass), and are therefore not normally distributed, thus breaking an assumption of analysis of variance. Angoff and Ford (1973) therefore suggest a transformed item difficulty model, where each item difficulty would be transformed algebraically to give a set of normally distributed equivalent values. This is done by finding the relative deviates that would cut off some proportion of the area under the normal curve. The distance from the common axis would then be plotted for the two groups (on a plot of group 1 against group 2) and used as an indicator of bias. Lord (1977), however, showed that this method was invalid unless the item characteristic curves are normal ogives and have the same discrimination (as in the Rasch model). Guessing also has a confounding effect.

An alternative approach to statistical tests for item bias is to compare the point biserial correlation coefficients between the item and the total score for the two groups, or to compare factor analyses for the two groups, but these approaches are still inexact where there are differences in the item characteristic curves (see Chapter 4). The chi-square approach (Scheuneman 1980) examines frequencies of correct response for two groups at different levels of test score, say by dividing into quartiles. This technique, although relatively free from error, is not particularly powerful. Finally, there are some exact models of item bias which carry out a direct comparison of the shape of the item characteristic curves obtained for each item within the two groups. All of these models are reviewed by Peterson (1980). In fact, where an item is clearly biased, it should show up whichever approach is used, and the models are likely to disagree only in borderline cases. When eliminating biased items, pragmatic considerations are usually more important than issues of whether the exact processes of the hypothetico-deductive model have been followed. Thus it may be advisable to use the easiest or more straightforward of these approaches (the analysis of variance or the chi square), even where their conclusions may not be exact. The approach used by Scheuneman (1975) in her demonstration of bias in the Otis-Lennon School Ability Test and the Metropolitan Reading Test was the chi-square technique.

Item offensiveness

An issue related to item bias is that of item offensiveness. This is not the same thing, as many offensive items can be unbiased, and many biased items may appear inoffensive. Thus the well-known Stanford-Binet item where the child is asked to say which of two pictures of a girl or boy is ugly, and which attractive, can be offensive to people who are not conventionally attractive; however, it has not been shown to be biased in any way. There are very good reasons for eliminating offensive items other than the fact that they may interfere with performance on the subsequent items in the test. Items which may be seen as sacrileges should obviously be avoided, as should items with irrelevant sexual connotations.

Racism and sexism must be avoided, and it should be remembered that items which draw attention to prejudice can often be as disturbing as items which exhibit it. Examples here might be the use of anti-semitic passages from Dickens or Shakespeare within English literature examinations. The use of stereotypes, for example men and women within traditional male and female roles, convey expectations about what is normal and should also be eliminated.

Intrinsic test bias

Intrinsic test bias exists where a test shows differences in the mean score of two groups which are due to the characteristics of the test and not to any difference between the groups in the trait or function being measured. It can be due to the test having different reliability for the two groups, or to group differences in the validity of the test (e.g., the same trait being measured in different proportions in the two groups, the measurement of an additional trait in one group, the measurement of unique traits in each group, or the test measuring nothing in common when applied to the two groups). Thus, for example, if a general knowledge test was administered in English to two groups, one of which was fluent in English while the other included people with a wide range of competences in English language, then while the test may be measuring general knowledge in one group, it would be highly contaminated by a measure of competency in English in the other group. The validities in the two groups would thus be different.

Intrinsic test bias can also be due to bias in the criterion against which the predictive power of the test is validated. For example, if university degree class marks were biased against overseas students, then a selection test for admission to university which used degree class as the criterion for its predictive validation would also tend to be biased. In practice intrinsic test bias is a matter of degree.

Differential content and predictive validity are the main causes of intrinsic test bias. Thus a test which has been constructed to match the characteristics of successful applicants from one particular group may not be so valid when applied to another. Differential content validity is the most worrying form of this bias as deviations in content validity are particularly likely to produce lower test scores in deviating groups. Any group on which the specification for a test has been constructed tends to perform better on that test than rival groups. This is because the cells of the specification, and thus groups of items within the test, will have been drawn up with people from this group in mind. If for some reason a cell or group of items is not properly applicable to another group, then inevitably members of that group would be expected to get lower scores. Several statistical models of intrinsic test bias in selection have been produced to eliminate bias, and these attracted a great deal of attention in the early 1970s as they seemed to provide a rationale for the positive discrimination programmes which were becoming popular at that time. There are two basic models of positive discrimination as seen from the statistical standpoint, first the use of different cut-off points and second the use of quotas.

Statistical models of intrinsic test bias

Cleary (1968) noted that a common regression equation usually under-predicted criterion scores for minorities, giving examples from data on black students' scores in integrated colleges in the USA. Cleary presented a model which allowed for different regression equations for each group when using the equation to predict, from test scores, the performance of two groups on a criterion ($y = A + Bx$, with A and B both being different for the two groups). This is illustrated in Figure 6.1. It was argued that true fairness had to be based on the use of the best predictor available. Effectively what was done was to equate the groups in terms of the cut-off point on the criterion, which, as the two predictive equations were different, produced different group cut-offs on the test score. Thus, suppose the cut-offs in the use of a test for selection for a course were 50 for group 1 and 60 for group 2. All persons in group 1 with scores higher than 50 would be selected, as would be all persons in group 2 with scores higher than 60. However, persons in group 2 who obtained scores between 50 and 60 would not be selected, even though their colleagues with these scores in group 1 would. They may well feel this was unfair, but the strong statistical argument here would be that they were mistaken and had failed to understand what selection was about. As the scores on the criterion had been equated, it would be argued, the score of 60 in group 2 was in fact equivalent to a score of 50 in group 1, and therefore no unfairness had occurred. Clearly here we have a difference of opinion based on the differences between the statistical and the traditional notions of fairness. Issues of this type were widely tested in the courts of the USA during the 1970s, where psychometricians representing the state or employers were asked to put their case against lawyers representing clients who took recourse to

Figure 6.1: Adjustment for intrinsic test bias using separate regression equations.

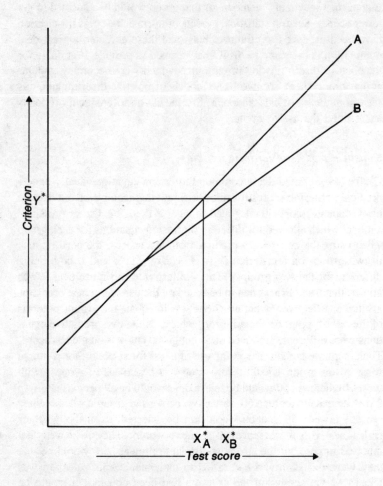

Equation A is represented by straight line A for Group A. Equation B is represented by straight line B for group B. The same performance on the criterion at y^* (the selection cut-off) is equivalent to scores above x^*_A for group A members, and to scores above x^*_B for group B members.

notions of justice contained in the United States Constitution. Thus in the case of Bakke v. the Regents of the University of California Medical School (1977), Bakke, a white student who had been refused a place in the medical school on the basis of a test score higher than that of some of his black fellow applicants, argued that his civil rights under the constitution, which guaranteed him equality regardless of race, had been breached. The case was carried by the Supreme Court of California, and eventually by the US Supreme Court, where a 5 to 4 majority verdict ruled in his favour. However, the judgment was not unanimous, and an appendix gave some clarification. It was ruled that, while the medical school had violated the equal protection clause of the US Constitution in this particular case, affirmative action programmes generally did not do so unless selection was merely on grounds of race. Had the medical school used a positive discrimination programme which looked at social or educational deprivation rather than race, then the ruling would not apply. Over the years the complex two-way interaction between the US courts and the test constructors has led to increased rigour and accountability in the use of tests, which are generally now of a much higher quality.

From the statisticians' viewpoint much of this legal argument might have been seen as irrelevant. Howver, this particular 'holier-than-thou' position was dealt a considerable blow by the development of alternative models of intrinsic test bias. Einhorn and Bass (1971) produced a threshold loss function model for the prediction from the regression lines for the two groups, and argued that Cleary's mean square error function model was not appropriate. This model allowed for differences in error term between the equations for the two groups, as well as for the usual alpha and beta regression functions ($y = A + Bx + E$, rather than $y = A + Bx$, with E, as well as A and B, being different for the two groups). While this represented an interesting academic difference of opinion, its practical consequences were devastating to the statisticians' case. Had the statisticians had a single viewpoint to set against popular notions of fairness, they might well have persuaded people of the correctness of their position. However, it was quite different to expect people to accept that they might be selected for a job if psychometricians chose to use a mean square error function, but not if they used a threshold loss function!

More new models confused rather than clarified the issue. Darlington (1971) produced the modified criterion model, which he claimed maximized validity and did not involve a quota system. Thorndike (1971) gave a constant ratio model in which groups were selected in ratio to their success on the criterion. He argued that the cut-off point should select groups in proportion to the fraction reaching specified levels of criterion performance. The conditional probability model of Cole (1973) based the probability of selection on the idea that all applicants who would be successful if accepted should have an equal chance of acceptance. Gross and Su (1975) produced a threshold utility model which used statistical decision theory to incorporate social factors directly into the decision process. This model accepted applicants with the highest expected utility. Utility was defined in terms of a statistical estimate of the social usefulness of having members of particular groups selected.

The models generally had no common criteria, and indeed some of the criteria were contradictory. It seems to be impossible to generate a model which is both fair to groups and fair to individuals. The fairer the models become with respect to groups the less fair they are for individuals, and vice versa. Some of the models resulted in a quota system, while others did not, and all could lead to some individuals being rejected who had higher scores than accepted individuals. A common tendency with them all was the identification of disadvantage with lower scoring on the test, the use of a mechanical formula, and the implicit matching of disadvantage with ethnicity rather than relying on direct measurement. Each of these characteristics has led to its own problems. The identification of disadvantage with low score causes particular problems where the disadvantaged group actually tends to have a higher score on the test. The use of the model in these circumstances, which are often found in cases of sex inequality, can lead to a decrease rather than an increase in the number of women being selected. Yet not to apply the formula or use the technique on a post hoc basis in these circumstances would show the procedure to be an excuse for action, rather than the rational and systematic method that it is claimed to be. The matching of disadvantage with ethnicity has also generated problems in circumstances where such a match is partially invalid.

A further problem with the techniques for adjusting intrinsic test bias has been that, even with their use, the most disadvantaged were still not being selected. Interest in all of these models decreased as it was increasingly realized that, in most cases of serious discrimination, the source of bias was extrinsic to the tests themselves.

Extrinsic test bias

Extrinsic test bias is found when decisions leading to inequality are made following the use of the test, but where the test itself is not biased. This can occur when two different groups have different scores on a test due to actual differences between the groups. Thus the use of the test, although itself unbiased, still results in a disproportionate selection of one group at the expense of the other. This situation is much more common in practice than intrinsic test bias, and is often the consequence of social deprivation. Thus an immigrant group which lives in a deprived inner city area where the schools are of poor quality is unlikely to generate many successes in terms of the academic qualifications of its children. The lack of these qualifications does not necessarily represent any bias in the examination but is more likely due to lack of opportunity. Where the community suffers deprivation for several generations the lack of opportunity is reflected in a lack of encouragement by parents, and a cycle of deprivation can easily be established.

Extrinsic test bias and ideology

There are two scientific and political groups likely to oppose the concept of extrinsic test bias. First, sociobiologists are likely to argue that differences in test scores between groups are in fact due to genetic differences between the two groups, and therefore do not represent bias so much as true differences. Second, extremely right-wing individuals may not see differences between cultural groups as undesirable, and are therefore unlikely to recognize them as bias. This controversy illustrates that bias is social and political in nature. What appears to be bias in one framework may not be so in another. However, it would be a mistake to imagine the possibility of an atheoretical framework, free from ideology, in which issues of bias could be rationally debated, leading to ideology-free notions of bias. Conceptions of unfairness, including conceptions of bias, are one of the corner stones of ideology itself, and issues of ideology are implicit in any consideration of bias. Psychometricians need to be prepared to make a stand on these issues before they can proceed to offer solutions. Any ideological issues which are substantially involved in the selection or assessment process are relevant to the psychometrician's task, and any form of test bias which can result in social inequality must be a central concern.

Legal aspects of extrinsic test bias

As with issues of intrinsic bias, there have been many judicial cases, particularly in the USA, which have considered the various points of view on the use of tests in situations of extrinsic bias. The most well known of these is that of Larry P. v. Wilson Ryles, Superintendent of Instruction for the State of California. This case came about as the result of the placement of seven black children into educational remedial classes on the basis of a WISC score of less than 75. The main case put forward by the parents was based on evidence that, while 9.1% of the catchment area was composed of black people, the proportion of black children in educational remedial classes was 27.5%. The ruling, in favour of the parents, included the principle that the burden of proof for non-bias rests with the test users, so that in these circumstances it was not up to the parents to prove that there was bias, but up to the California education department to prove that there was not bias. As a consequence no black children in California may be placed in educational remedial classes on the basis of IQ tests if the consequence is racial imbalance. In 1979, IQ tests which did this were ruled unconstitutional by the Californian courts. Another case, that of Diana v. the California State Board of Education, was settled out of course. Since 1979 the use of the WISC has been outlawed in many American states, and has fallen into disrepute in most others.

What is particularly important about all of these cases is that they emphasize the need to make any sources of bias explicit, and to incorporate remedial factors into any selection or assessment programme. Extrinsic test bias can be identified by observing the existence of any form of disadvantage which is continuing or deteriorating in situations where testing has been involved in selection or assessment. Once extrinsic bias has been demonstrated, it is not sufficient to ignore its basis, or its role in a society which includes disadvantaged groups. One common solution is the introduction of special access courses to provide added educational input. An alternative approach is the reformulation of the curriculum objectives or job specification to eliminate biased components which may be irrelevant or relatively insignificant when put against the wider need for an equitable society.

The importance of test validity was also demonstrated by the case of Griggs v. Duke Power Station, where it was ruled that the power station had failed to demonstrate that the Wonderlic Personnel Test they used in their promotion procedures was actually relevant to the tasks which employees were expected to carry out. Another relevant case is that of the Albemarle Paper Company v. Moody, in which it was again ruled that the test user must demonstrate the validity of the tests used; it was not up to the testee to demonstrate the evidence for invalidity. In the case of Armstead et al. v. Starkeville School District, the Graduate Record Examination (GRE) was ruled to be inappropriate.

Guidelines in cases of test bias

The US equal opportunity commission has issued guidelines for selectors in situations prone to extrinsic test bias. They argue that affirmative action programmes should in general de-emphasize race, and emphasize instead the educational level of the parents, the relative educational level of the peer group, the examination level, the quality of schooling, and the availability of compensatory facilities. They further recommend job re-specification, the introduction of specific training programmes, and the equalization of numbers of applications by changing advertising strategies.

Summary

Three ways in which psychometric tests can be biased have been described. Item bias has proved to be the most amenable to direct amendment. Intrinsic test bias has received a very wide consideration by psychometricians and policy makers alike with the result that today the use of any test in the USA must be accompanied by positive proof that it is not biased in this way. Issues of extrinsic test bias have lead to a much closer collaboration between psychometricians and policy makers generally, and to a recognition that ideological issues are of fundamental importance to the theoretical basis of psychometrics. The political links between psychometrics and popular conceptions of democracy continue to develop through the legal structure at both legislative and individual case level in many countries.

Chapter seven

The profile and graded testing

While the consideration of selection tests can be the most instructive way in which to approach many psychometric issues, not all psychometric tests are used for selection. In some of these non-selective situations, such as the use of tests in assessment, special considerations apply. Even in the use of selective tests it is not always appropriate to proceed by the use of the standard model. One special case is in examinations held for licensing procedures for professional bodies. When a person is licensed to practise a profession it is often not the case that a complete specification of the job forms the basis of the examinations used. Often the function of these examinations can not be clearly defined, and the test score has developed several different, indeed sometimes contradictory, uses through evolving social convention. Thus the General Certificate of Education O level in English or mathematics is often required by employers for any variety of circumstances, even though it was originally constructed to academic criteria. The GCE A level in particular has clearly been aimed at preparation for the university syllabus, even though most successful candidates do not in the end follow the particular syllabus involved. It could be argued here that the GCE results are being misused by employers, and that a more appropriate examination for their use should be devised. However, this presents some difficulties, as the actual needs of every employer are different, while there are common educational issues which determine what should be included in an examination, particularly in relation to its role in defining and controlling the curriculum.

Alternative approaches to school examinations

Since the 1960s, the idea that school examinations should be more than mere selective devices for university admission has led to a serious rethinking of their function in society in general. However, their role had become so embroiled in standard selection practice that attempts to shift the system proved unsuccessful until the 1980s. Teachers had been concerned for some time about the deadening impact that the GCE syllabus was having on the educational motivation of the less able. In many schools in deprived inner city areas very few children were reaching the standards required by these examinations, so that most were leaving school with no certificates at all. However, their education was still controlled by the GCE syllabus, which was geared to the academic approach to school learning. The introduction of the CSE was intended to overcome many of these problems but was largely unsuccessful, as the new examination was widely seen as a second-class qualification, a sign of failure at GCE O level rather than of success at CSE level. It was generally felt within these schools that a much closer integration of the syllabus with the examination was the only way in which it would be possible to give meaningful accreditation to the less able children. In 1987 a new system, the GCSE, was introduced with the aim of abolishing the distinction between CSE and GCE and providing a continuous scale.

Continuous assessment and formative assessment

Integration of curriculum and assessment has led to two major developments in the examination system. First, the introduction of continuous assessment into the certificated examination within first the CSE and then the GCSE has involved teachers much more closely in the process of certification. Second, a distinction between formative assessment, where assessment is carried out to enable the child to monitor and improve his or her own learning, and summative assessment, a certificated result at the end of schooling for prospective employers, has led to a weakening of the influence of the examination boards on curriculum control. While the emphasis was on performance in a final examination, one of the main concerns of the teacher was bound to be the need for pupils to obtain high marks in that examination. The writers of the examination in these circumstances therefore effectively controlled the curriculum. As the examination became less important this control slackened.

The changes in educational assessment techniques, while of benefit to teachers and the learning process, have not met with widespread approval among higher education establishments and employers. The latter in particular have expressed concern about the educational standards of the school leavers they have recruited, even though to date most of these have in fact been from the old system rather than the new. The question of accreditation of school leavers has complex ideological ramifications. From some political perspectives, the major purpose of state education is seen to be the generation of people with the skills needed for industry, the 'factory fodder' model. From other points of view, the aim of education is the encouragement of the pupils' self-respect and their ability to find things out for themselves. However, from neither of these points of view is it particularly desirable that employers should need to produce their own examinations, or that private employment organizations should take over from schools the task of accreditation for employment. Any new examination system will, therefore, need to continue to provide the role of the old GCE in providing evidence of literacy and numeracy for employers. As more parties were brought into the debate, the area of argument widened. By the late 1980s examination and accreditation procedures within the British school system were in turmoil.

One of the major concerns was that something should be done for those who had previously left the educational system with no accreditation at all. Two ideas were introduced to help such people. First, the introduction of criterion referencing rather than norm referencing (see Chapter 3) of examination items might emphasize what a pupil could actually do without the need to make a comparison with other children and, second, the introduction of pupil profiles would show where the pupil's strengths might lie, as well as weaknesses.

Profiles

The use of profiles has a long history in psychometrics. Indeed they do seem particularly suited to this new task, as they have generally been designed to present an overall picture of an individual for judgmental or diagnostic procedures, rather than for simple success or failure. Within a profile, not one but many test scores are presented, but in such a way that they can be compared with each other. These are called sub-tests, and there can often be items from as many as 20 sub-tests randomly mixed up within a single questionnaire, with the items only being brought together for scoring purposes. Raw sub-scale scores need to be standardized, and the set of standardized sub-scale scores are then illustrated on a profile sheet, which will have a sub-scale score as the y axis, usually with stanine scores ranging from 1 to 9 with 5 as the mid-point, and the various sub-scales laid out along the x axis. An example of a profile is given in Figure 7.1.

The Minnesota Multiphasic Personality Inventory (MMPI)

One of the earliest profile systems developed was the Minnesota Multiphasic Personality Inventory (MMPI), which is still in use today and which provides a good general example of the technique. The MMPI was developed as a broad spectrum personality test to be used on psychiatric patients, usually on admission to psychiatric hospital. It consists of over 200 personality test style items (of the type: Are you a nervous person? Do you sometimes hear voices? Are there enemies who are out to get you? etc.), which form a set of sub-tests within the overall questionnaire. Within the MMPI there are sub-tests of hypochon-driasis, depression, hysteria, psychopathy, paranoia, psychoasthenia, schizophrenia, hypomania and masculinity-femininity. These sub-tests are each scored separately, and each is subjected to separate standard-ization. An individual's MMPI sub-scale scores are entered as points on a graph, and the points joined to form a profile. On such a profile, areas which are particularly problematic will appear as peaks on the graph, the higher the peak the greater being the disturbance. Psychiatrists who see large numbers of such profiles on their patients will soon begin to recognize common patterns, representing well-known conditions, such as for example paranoid schizophrenia.

Expert use of profiles can save a clinician a great deal of time. Obvious disorders stand out easily, difficulties are immediately made apparent, and the data are summarized in a standard and accepted way for all clinicians. While the ways in which profiles are used by professionals depend on the use of judgment, with the instrument as a tool for helping an essentially human process, the same principles of reliability, validity and proper standardization apply to each of the sub-scales as would apply to a single longer scale. Thus the proper psychometric construction of a profiling system is a much more complex and time consuming process than constructing a single test.

Figure 7.1 An example of a diagnostic profile taken from the Golombok Rust Inventory of Sexual Satisfaction (GRISS).

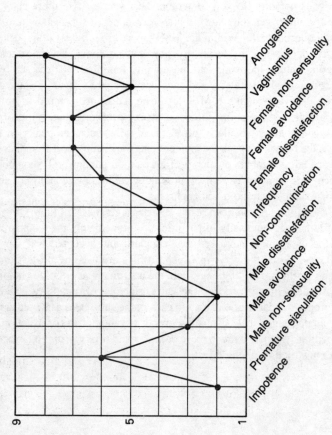

Twelve subscales have transformed scores of 1 to 9, with 5 and above indicating a problem. This particular profile is for a couple attending a sexual dysfunction clinic.

Profiles in schools

The conceptual model for the application of profiles within education is in many ways equivalent to their use in the MMPI. Rather than a restricted set of academic subjects, the sub-tests of the profile sometimes include elements from all areas of the child's educational achievement, including moral and behavioural evaluations and extracurricular activities. Each pupil will have a score on each sub-test, so that evaluation will take place at some level for every aspect of the domain. Early attempts at developing pupil profiles also laid particular emphasis on behavioural criterion related items, which were seen as emphasizing what the child could actually do, rather than how the child compared with his or her peers. The City and Guilds of London was one of the first establishments to make use of profiles of this type. Their profiles provide a good illustration of the problem of profiling in this manner. One of their model profiles includes sub-scale categories of communication (comprised of the sub-scales of talking and listening, reading and writing, and using signs and diagrams), social abilities (working in a group, working with those in authority, working with clients), practical and numerical abilities (using equipment, control of movement, measuring, and calculating), and decision making abilities (planning, seeking information, coping, and assessing results). In their sub-scale for calculating, for example, they have five categories representing five levels of achievement. These are: can count; can add and subtract whole numbers; can use multiplication and division to solve whole number problems; can add and subtract decimals and simple fractions; and can multiply and divide decimals and simple fractions. The criteria relatedness of all these categories is admirable; however, there is one very immediate problem: while the profile indicates clearly what the pupil can do, it also makes all too apparent what the pupil cannot do. An employer reading the results from the criterion related scale would tend to perceive that a person who can add and subtract whole numbers is also someone who is unable to multiply and divide or to deal with fractions and decimals. While in an ideal world the employer may think this irrelevant to the job in hand, it is unlikely to be ignored if other job applicants can achieve these additional skills. Consider also the five response categories for reading and writing: can read short sentences; can read and write messages; can follow and give straight-forward written instructions and explanations; can use instruction manuals and can write reports describing work done; and can select and criticize written data and use them to produce own written work. There is a whole set of hidden messages in these categories. For example, does 'can read short sentences' in this context mean that the person is unable to write? And if so, has not the employer the right to be told this directly?

The success and failure of pupil profiles

The attempts to include life skills and moral development within pupil profiles have been even more fraught. Very few authorities have taken the conception to its logical limit and included scales on honesty. One of the main problems with profiles of this type is in fact an ethical one. By increasing the capacity of the scheme to say something positive about everyone, we are also enabling more negative information to be conveyed. If it is desired that pupil assessments should give the opportunity for a person's honesty to be reported, then by default, if it is not reported there is the implication of dishonesty. There are two dangers here which are contradictory. If the assessment scheme is inaccurate, then there is the serious risk of injustice and libel; on the other hand, if the assessment scheme is accurate and known to be so, then what chances in life would a school leaver have if a reputation for dishonesty was included on their final school report? It is probably generally felt that there are some aspects of a person's performance, particularly during growing up, that individuals have a right to keep secret. As computerized databases come to have more impact on our lives, the dangers of abuse for the type of information provided by school leaving profiles are considerable.

The main problem with reliable and valid psychometric pupil profiles was really that they were just too good. Far more information can be conveyed than is necessarily in the child's interest. Rather than considering the implications of this in an honest and straightforward manner, in practice various disingenuous strategies have unfortunately been developed for coping with these dangers of over exposure. In the early 1980s there tended to be a denial of the necessity for psychometric techniques such as validation, as if data of the profile type, when criterion related, somehow escaped the need to be reliable and valid. It was suggested that, with formative assessment in particular, the new subject of 'edumetrics' should replace the ideologically unsound psychometrics of the past, and lead to a new science of assessment. There seemed to be a blindness to the fact that the need for reliable and valid data emerged from the need for reliable and valid processes. It is a complete nonsense to believe that, merely because the sociobiological approach to intelligence testing emphasized the reliability and validity of IQ tests, reliability and validity are somehow no longer an acceptable part of psychometrics. They are as central to it as they have ever been.

The second strategy involved attempts to report the data selectively. Thus an employer when given the results of the profile might merely be told that the pupil can read short sentences and can count. The further crucial information that he was unable to write or add up and subtract would not be given. Now of course an employer familiar with the scheme might be able to make this deduction; however, later developments in profiling attempted to prevent this by rewriting the information in the style of a personal reference rather than an examination result. This procedure can be easily computerized, with the positive items from the profile being transformed into various grammatical alternatives, the name of the pupil being substituted for X, and pronoun adjustments (his or her) being made automatically. Thus, the program might report, 'Maureen has ability at reading sentences, especially if they are short. She is also particularly good at counting.' This example is, of course, somewhat extreme but not an improbable outcome of this type of system. If such a scheme is introduced it is only a matter of time before employers become as proficient at reading these profiles as they currently need to be at interpreting written references and testimonials.

But is this the most productive direction for our examination system? In spite of the obvious difficulties of such an approach, the achievement by 1990 of a national system of school leaving profiles, now called 'records of achievement', is national policy in England and Wales. The reasons, however, are political rather than ideological or even pedagogic. The purposes of the scheme as laid out in the 1984 Department of Education and Science Policy Statement, while including the recognition of achievement and the need for a short, clear and concise summary document valued by employers, emphasizes the role of the formative profile in motivation and personal development, as well as in curriculum and organizational review. In fact the use of profiles in formative assessment, by allowing for continuous monitoring across the whole range of activities, provided an ideal instrument of curriculum control for both national and local government alike. Formative assessment of pupils necessarily has to involve the teachers, and in the process of instructing teachers in its methods a great deal of control of the curriculum passes to their instructors. It is to this new ground that the curriculum control shifts as soon as final examinations are downgraded in their significance. The political debate between the left, who would like to see this control used to introduce a multicultural curriculum, and the right who would like to see a system of industrially orientated skills training introduced, will no doubt continue for some years.

The standard profile contains one essential characteristic: it must include a series of measures or sub-scales. While the assignment to points on these sub-scales may often be criterion referenced rather than norm referenced, it must, if it is to be able to state what a person can do, by default tell us what a person cannot do. Incomplete reporting can obscure this but not eliminate it. In fact there are many instances of profile reporting which have not traditionally been seen as profiling. When an individual's O and A level scores are reported, we have a set of scores on a series of sub-scales, and we make comparisons of clusters of successful and unsuccessful subjects. The manner in which we plan out a reference, deciding to say something about ability, how hard the person works, how they get on with other people, etc., is again an example of an implicit profile structure. This might suggest that profiling, rather than being a psychometric technique introduced by the advance of science, is merely an operationalization of folk psychological decision making processes so far as they apply to judging and assessing other human individuals.

Graded tests

Ideas drawn from criterion referencing, in particular the evaluation of behavioural skills, have also had an impact on the policy of the Department of Education and Science in the UK on the nature of their new GCSE system recently introduced in England and Wales. Here, as with the record of achievements, the approach has been politically inspired and consequently includes aspects which are likely to fall apart as soon as practical considerations arise. Graded tests, such as those used for assessing ability on the piano, have often been held up as a model of good testing practice. While the inspiration provided by the success of graded tests is to be welcomed, most subjects taught in schools cannot be graded in any simple manner. The mastery of a musical instrument, or a skill such as driving a car, is in many ways a false analogy for achievement in subjects such as geography, history, mathematics and science. Attempts to establish grade criteria are likely either to meet an ignoble end, or else be pseudo-criterion based, being in effect norm driven from the teachers' knowledge of the usual performance, understanding and learning rates of their pupils. It is unfortunate that the criterion related issue was ever introduced into the school examination system in this way.

The definition of success in a subject and in its application is a complex issue which is more properly judged in terms of the traditional concept of validity than in terms of some exaggerated contradiction between norm and criterion referencing. The level at which psychometric issues have been judged within the British school system over recent years should be a matter for considerable embarrassment.

A recent controversy over grading at A level showed alarming levels of ignorance among the educationists responsible for the examination system as well as among politicians and parents. Following reports in the press, it was felt that the B and D grade were 'too close together' in terms of raw marks, and there was a demand that they should be 'moved further apart'. Of course, everybody would like the marking system to be as accurate as possible, but when there are too many good applicants for too few places there are bound to be mistakes made, particularly near the cut-off. But this would be the case however people were selected. The solution can only be to make the selection more accurate or to increase the number of places. Tinkering with the mark to grade transformations to give a larger proportion of B grades will not achieve anything unless more university places are available. However, once the point had been made and political stances on the issue established, a face saving formula had to be introduced for redefining numerical to grade transformations within the A, B and C grade. The damage done to the credibility of the system has yet to be repaired. It seems that where politicians of left and right have a common interest in the introduction of 'new-speak', reason is the first fatality.

Neuropsychological assessment

An example of a successfully applied profiling system can be given from the use of neuropsychological testing in the assessment of brain dysfunction. The use of profiles here grew out of a practical need by the medical community to describe more completely the behavioural effects of brain damage. These behavioural data could then act as part of the diagnostic assessment of the severity and localization of brain lesions. As a further advantage it was non-obtrusive, and it could also provide a technique for monitoring improvement after treatment. There have traditionally been two major systems in use, the Halstead-Reitan Batteries (Reitan 1955), and the Luria-Nebraska Neuropsychological Test Battery (Golden et al. 1978). The Halstead-Reitan Batteries were almost completely functional and quantitative in their origin, and amounted to a formalization and agreement among clinicians on the set of sub-tests which were appropriate for diagnosis of brain damage. The battery included existing scales, such as the Wechsler Adult Intelligence Scale (Wechsler 1958) as well as new or adapted tests. The sub-test domains include concept formation, abstraction and integration; tactual discrimination, manual dexterity, kinaesthesis, incidental memory, spatial memory, verbal auditory discrimination, auditory visual integration, phonetic skills; non-verbal auditory discrimination, auditory perception; motor speed, visual scanning, visual motor integration, mental flexibility, integration of alphabetic and numeric systems; and motor speed dexterity. Adjunct tests often used were the WAIS or WISC, the MMPI, and tests of lateral dominance. The interpretation of these complex profiles to produce a diagnosis was traditionally carried out by expert judgment, and would also take into account adjustments for age, socio-economic background, sex, chronicity and any other factors which were felt to be relevant. However, in spite of the strong judgmental element in the interpretation, psychometric criteria were of prime importance in establishing the reliability and validity of the sub-tests themselves.

It was felt by the 1960s that many of the tests included in the Halstead-Reitan Battery were rather ad hoc, and the sub-tests of intellectual functioning in particular reflected a hotch potch of often contradictory underlying theories. While the profile had been found to be effective for diagnostic purposes, advances in brain science generally were suggesting that a battery based on an overall understanding of brain functioning was now a plausible possibility. The first major diagnostic system to involve such a global theory was that of Luria (1973); however, this was qualitative in nature. After several aborted attempts at quantification the Luria-Nebraska System was the first to gain widespread acceptance. Luria's model distinguishes areas of motor function, an acoustic-motor rhythm scale, a higher cutaneous kinaesthetic tactile scale, spatial visual functions, a receptive speech scale, an expressive speech scale, and scales of reading, arithmetic, memory and intellectual functioning.

Both these batteries form an important part of the diagnostic work of neuropsychologists, brain scientists and clinicians. They have been particularly successful in diagnosing brain damage in 18–45 year olds. Difficulties are encountered with children (where the constant presence of developmental change always makes medical diagnosis difficult), and in older people, where the effects of brain damage become confounded with the mental deterioration of the normal ageing process.

Summary

There is a demand for psychometric tests not only in selection but also in clinical or educational assessment. Within these latter settings additional criteria can apply to their construction and use. In educational settings the complex interaction between the curriculum and the test specification in situations where assessment is continuous has led to new understandings in the approach to both. In the clinical setting, the power of psychometric procedures within a single diagnosis has led to a high degree of sophistication and refinement in particular techniques such as profiling.

Chapter eight

Factor analysis

Factor analysis is a technique which is widely used in psychometrics. It can be applied to any set of data where the number of subjects exceeds the number of variables, and is normally carried out on a computer. The variables involved in the use of factor analysis are usually item scores or sub-test scores. The analysis will provide a set of results which give an indication of the underlying relationships between the items or sub-tests. It will tell us which set of items or sub-tests go together, and which stand apart. Factor analysis identifies what are called 'factors' in the data. These factors are underlying hypothetical constructs which often can be used to explain the data. Factor analytic computer programs will give an estimate of how many such factors there may be in a set of data, and of how these factors relate to the items or sub-tests. By selecting items which relate to particular factors we are able to put together sub-tests of the construct that the factor represents. Factor analytic computer programs also give eigenvalues, statistics which are able to represent the relative importance of a factor, and can give estimates of the scores of individuals on any of the factors identified.

The correlation coefficient

One statistic which is fundamental to psychometrics and occurs again and again, is the correlation coefficient. When a test is constructed, we correlate item scores with total scores to obtain discrimination in the item analysis (see Chapter 4), we calculate correlations to obtain the reliability (see Chapter 5), and sometimes we use them for validity estimation as well. In addition, if we have a series of sub-tests the correlation between them is of interest as it is useful to know the extent to which they are measuring the same concept. This is also essential if we are to be able to make proper use of a profile analysis. And finally, the use of a test score itself often involves correlation with another variable.

The correlation matrix

Correlations are often summarized within a correlation matrix (see Table 8.1). For an item analysis we can imagine correlations between all the items 'a', 'b', 'c', 'd', 'e', 'f', and so on. If we draw a matrix with both the rows and columns labelled 'a', 'b', 'c', etc., then where the rows and columns meet within the body of the matrix we can write a correlation.

Table 8.1 A correlation matrix, representing correlations between the various components of an EEG evoked potential

	P2L	N2L	P3L	N3L	P2−N2	N2−P3
N2L	0.66					
P3L	0.07	0.18				
N3L	−0.04	0.09	0.25			
P2−N2	−0.04	−0.05	−0.29	−0.22		
N2−P3	−0.02	−0.06	−0.25	−0.14	0.86	
P3−N3	0.13	0.03	−0.21	−0.06	0.36	0.58

From Rust, J. (1975), 'Genetic effects in the auditory cortical evoked potential: a twin study', *Electroencephalography and Clinical Neurophysiology*, 39(4), 321-7.

Thus where row 'b' crosses column 'c' we have the correlation between 'b' and 'c', where row 'b' crosses column 'b' we have the correlation of 'b' with itself (which will always be 1), where row 'c' crosses column 'b' we will have the correlation between 'b' and 'c' again. In fact it is easy to see that all possible correlations between each of the items in the matrix will occur twice. The statistical analysis of correlation matrices uses matrix algebra and forms the basis of much of multivariate statistics. However, the basic structure of these matrices has been of interest to psychologists since the turn of the century when Charles Spearman developed the technique of factor analysis, the first attempt to look for some underlying uniformity in the structure of correlation matrices.

The statistics and algebra of factor analysis are complicated; however, there are alternative ways of looking at factor analysis than the purely mathematical. Graphic techniques (see Figure 8.1), which have produced visual representations of the process, have had a major impact on the development of psychometrics. These involve visualizations of the way in which variables relate to each other, and make the conceptualization of issues in psychometrics much easier. The basic ideas of factor analysis have emerged again and again in psychology, from multidimensional scaling in psychophysics to the interpretation of repertory grids in social and clinical psychology, but they are fundamentally based on the models provided by vector algebra. In vector algebra two values are ascribed to an object: force and direction. Within factor analytic models, variables are represented by the 'force' element of the vector, which is held constant at value 1, while the angle between two variables represents the correlation between them in such a manner that the cosine of this angle is equal to the Pearson product–moment correlation coefficient. Thus a correlation of 0.71 between variables 'a' and 'b' is represented by two lines of equal length with an angle between them whose cosine is 0.71, that is 45 degrees. The translation between cosines and angles can be made using cosine tables, which appear at the back of many mathematical or statistical texts. Cosine to angle transformation is also a normal push-button option on most scientific calculators.

Figure 8.1 Spatial representation of the correlation coefficient.

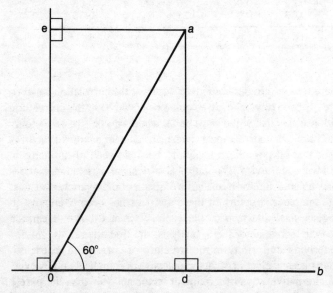

A correlation of 0.5 between two variables *a* and *b* can be represented graphically by two lines of the same length which have an angle whose cosine is 0.5 (60°) between them.

116

There are many useful characteristics which follow from this visual representation of the correlation. In Figure 8.1 we can see that one of the vectors 'ob' is drawn horizontally, and the other 'oa' above it is drawn at the appropriate angle AOB. A perpendicular 'ad' is then dropped on to 'ob' from 'a' to a point 'd'. If we assume that 'ob' and 'oa' have unit length, the distance 'od' will then be equal to the cosine of the angle between the vectors, and therefore to the correlation itself. Also in the figure we see that a vertical 'oe' at right angles to 'ob' has been drawn, and projected onto it is a horizontal line 'ae'. By Pythagoras we know that, as 'oa' has unit length, then 'od'^{2} + 'oe'^{2} = 1. This gives us a graphical restatement of the statistical formula $r^2 + (1 - r)^2 = 1$, which tells us how we can use the correlation coefficient to partition variance. To give an example, if the correlation between age and a measure of reading ability is 0.5, then we can say that 0.5^2, that is, 0.25 or 25%, of variance of reading ability is accounted for by age. It also follows that 75% of the variance in reading ability is not accounted for by age. This is represented graphically by drawing our lines 'oa' and 'ob' at an angle of 60° to each other as indeed is the case in the figure. The cosine of 60° is 0.5, and therefore, in our figure, the distance 'od' is 0.5. What is the distance 'oe'? Well, its square is 0.75 (the proportion based on the 75% variance we already know), so the distance 'oe' must be the square root of this, i.e. 0.866. This number can be seen as representing a correlation, but it is a correlation between reading ability and some hypothetical variable, as no vector 'oe' was originally given by the data. However, we can give a name to this variable; we could call it 'that part of reading ability which is independent of age'. We could estimate this value by partial correlation analysis, and we could use it in an experimental situation to eliminate age effects. While considering graphical representation of correlations, think about two special cases. If $r = 0$ and the variables are uncorrelated, the angle between 'oa' and 'ob' will be 90°, the cosine of 90° zero. The variables are thus each represented by their own spatial dimension. If $r = 1.0$, then the angle between 'oa' and 'ob' is zero (the cosine of 0° being 1.0) and they merge into a single vector. Thus the variables are graphically as well as statistically identical.

From this very simple conception we are able to demonstrate a fundamental idea of factor analysis: while the two lines 'oa' and 'ob' represent real variables, there is an infinite number of hidden variables which can exist in the same space, represented by lines drawn in any direction from 'o'. The hidden variable 'oe' represents an imaginary variable, that part of 'oa' which is independent of 'ob'. If 'oa' were, for example, the weight of a human being, and 'ob' was the height of a human being, then 'oe' would be that part of the variation in the weight of human beings which was independent of height. It is thus a measure of 'fatness', not measured directly but by measuring weight and height and applying an appropriate algorithm. There are any number of circumstances in which these models can be applied. Another example relevant to psychometrics may have 'ob' as the score on a psychological test and 'oa' as a measure of the criterion against which it is to be validated; thus the angle between 'oa' and 'ob', representing the correlation between 'a' (the test score) and 'b' (the criterion), becomes a measure of validity, and 'oe' becomes that aspect of the criterion which is not measured by the test.

A flat piece of paper, being two dimensional, is able to represent at most two totally independent sources of variation in any one figure. To extend this model to factor analysis we need to conceive not of one correlation but of a correlation matrix in which each variable is represented by a line of unit length from a common origin, and the correlations between the variables are represented by the angles between the lines. Taking first the simple case of three variables 'x', 'y' and 'z' (see Figure 8.2), and the three correlations between them, if the angle between 'ox' and 'oy' is 30°, that between 'oy' and 'oz' 30°, and that between 'ox' and 'oz' 60°, then it is quite easy to draw this situation on a piece of paper. This represents correlations of 0.87 (the cosine of 30°) between 'x' and 'y' and between 'y' and 'z', and a correlation of 0.5 (the cosine of 60°) between 'x' and 'z'.

However, if all these angles between 'ox', 'oy' and 'oz' were 30° this would be impossible — it would be necessary to conceive of one of the lines projecting into a third dimension to represent such a matrix. With more than three variables it may be that as many dimensions as variables are required to 'draw' the full matrix, or it may be that some reduction is possible. Factor analysis seeks to find the minimum number of dimensions required to satisfactorily describe all the data from the matrix. Sometimes matrices can be reduced to one dimension, sometimes two, three, four, five, and so on. Of course, there is always a certain amount of error in any measurement, so this reduction will always be a matter of degree. However, the models used will seek solutions which can simply describe as much variance as possible, and will then assume all else is error.

Figure 8.2 Figural representation of the correlations between three variables.

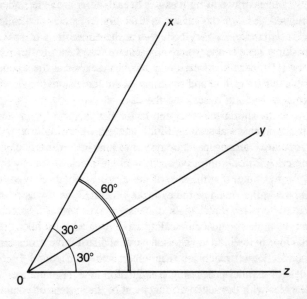

Variables represented are x, y & z, where the correlations between x and y, and between y and z are 0.87 (cosine = 30°), and that between x and z is 0.5 (cosine = 60°).

Thurstone (1947) developed one of the techniques for carrying out factor analysis within the vector model that has just been described. He extracted the first factor by the process of vector addition, which is in effect the same process as that for finding the centre of gravity in another application of vector algebra, and is thus called the centroid technique. The centroid is a 'hidden' variable, but it has the property that it describes more variance than any other dimension drawn through the multidimensional space, and we can in fact calculate this amount of variance by summing the squares of all the projections onto this vector from all the real variables. The square root of this value is called the eigenvalue of the factor. The position of the first factor can be described by reporting the correlation between it and each of the real variables, which are functions of the angles involved. The first factor within the centroid technique describes a basic fixing dimension, and when its position has been found it can be extracted from the multidimensional space so that further factors are sought only in regions at right angles to it. The cosine of an angle of 90°, that is of a right angle, is 0, and thus factors represented by lines drawn at right angles to each other are independent and uncorrelated. It is for this reason that factors are sometimes called dimensions, as figuratively they behave like the dimensions of space. A unidimensional scale is one which only requires one factor to describe it in this way. If further factors exist they will be described as the second, third, fourth and fifth factors and so on, and a unidimensional scale will not be adequate for fully describing the data.

There are many similarities between factor analysis and the process known as multidimensional scaling. Multidimensional scaling originally achieved popularity among psychophysicists, and proved particularly useful in practice for defining psychophysical variables. It was by this technique, for example, that the idea of there being only three types of colour receptor in the retina of the eye was generated, as it was found that people only required three colour dimensions to describe all colours. More recently, multidimensional scaling has provided a useful model for the behaviour of the hidden values in parallel distributive processing (PDP or connectionist) machines (Rumelhart and McClelland 1986). These models of parallel processing computation have been claimed to show similarities with the actual arrangement of the system of connections between neurones in the human brain (McClelland and Rumelhart 1987). If this is supported, then representational analogies of the type used in multidimensional scaling may turn out to be not just a convenient tool but to be closely related to higher cognitive processes at the information processing level. In much the same way in which multidimensional scaling models have provided a conceptual underpinning for psychophysics, factor analysis fulfils a similar role for psychometrics. Its success may be due to more than mere statistical convenience: it could be that the figural representation of factor analysis is so powerful because it mirrors the cognitive processes whereby human beings actually make judgments about differences between objects (or persons). It may therefore represent a fundamental principle of one aspect of cognitive science.

The application of factor analysis to test construction

In psychometric test construction the factor analysis of all the item correlations in a questionnaire provides an alternative technique to item analysis, and also provides additional information on the conceptual structure of the test specification and on forms of bias in the test. Because of the powerful number crunching ability of modern computers, it is relatively easy to carry out factor analysis, and many statistical packages carry it as one of their options. However, as factor analysis for psychologists has always been more of a conceptual tool than a statistical technique, there are dangers in the amateur use of these programs. While the statistical process of factor analysis is more or less automatic, there are many decisions about options and their defaults which need to be made along the way.

Finding the starting values for estimates of item error

In the absence of guidance the statistical programs operate default options, generally designed by statisticians rather than psychologists, and these can inadvertently mislead the user. The first set of these option sets provides the starting values for the iteration process used to fit the model. These starting values are in fact estimates of the extent to which each variable is contaminated by error, and are thus estimates of reliability. If reliabilities are known they can be entered directly, but if not then the program will have to estimate them, usually from either the largest correlation of the variable in question with any other, or from the average of its correlation with all of the others. It is useful to check these starting values to ensure that they are not spuriously high or low. A good way to do this is to run a principal components analysis on the data as well. This will usually be provided as an option within the factor analysis program. Principal components analysis has many similarities to factor analysis but was defined mathematically much earlier and does not give such a complete analysis. It is not strictly a statistical technique at all as there is no error term involved, and all variables are assumed to be completely reliable. If the principal components and factor analysis models produce more or less the same result then there is no special problem at this level. If on the other hand they give rather different results this will probably be due to large 'between item' variation in the estimates of item error. If this explanation makes sense then no adjustment to the factor analysis is necessary, but if it seems unrealistic it is probably advisable to insert better estimates of item reliability directly into the program. Most factor analysis programs allow this as an option.

Identifying the number of factors

The second point at which the default procedures intervene is the most troublesome: that of identifying the number of factors. The original factor analytic transformation generates as many factors as there are variables, and calculates an eigenvalue for each. The original set of variables defines the total amount of variance in the matrix, each variable contributing one unit. With a factor analysis of data on ten variables, therefore, the total amount of variance present will be 10. The factor analysis rearranges this variance and allocates a certain amount to each factor while conserving the total amount. The quantity allocated to each factor is a function of a statistic called the eigenvalue, and this is such that the sum of the squared eigenvalues of all the original factors adds up to the total number of variables. With 10 variables, for example, there will be 10 original factors. The sum of the squares of the eigenvalues of these factors will be 10, but individually they may vary between about 3 and little above zero. The larger the eigenvalue of a factor, the greater the amount of the total variance it accounts for, and the more important it is. The first factor will accumulate a fair amount of this common variance within its eigenvalue, and subsequent factors progressively less, so that some way along the line factors will begin to have eigenvalues of less than 1. Eigenvalues of less than 1 indicate that the factor is only able to account for a small amount of variance, in fact less than is accounted for by a single variable. As the purpose of factor analysis is to explain a large number of variables in terms of an underlying structure with fewer elements, factor eigenvalues of less than 1 are often interpreted as being uninteresting and probably due to error.

The Kaiser criterion for selecting the number of factors

Most factor analysis programs as a default accept only those factors whose eigenvalues are larger than 1 as being of interest. This is sometimes called the Kaiser criterion, and indeed it makes intuitive sense. However, this is not always so and fails in about 50% of cases. The major exceptions are (a) when there is too much noise in the system from too many unreliable variables, so that too many factors have eigenvalues greater than 1, and (b) when there are several factors with eigenvalues around the criterion level (usually 1). For example, it would not make much sense to use an eigenvalue criterion level of 1 where the eigenvalues for the first seven factors were 2.1, 1.8, 1.5, 1.1, 0.9, 0.6, 0.5. Although the Kaiser criterion would here give us four factors, it might make more sense to inspect either the three or the five factor solutions.

The Cattell 'scree' technique for identifying the number of factors

An alternative to Kaiser is provided by the so-called Cattell scree test, which uses the metaphor of the shingle on a sea shore for the shape of a plot of eigenvalue against factor number, and suggests that a scree might be expected just at the point before the noise values become operative.

Figure 8.3 Plot of eigenvalue against factor number demonstrating a Cattell 'scree'.

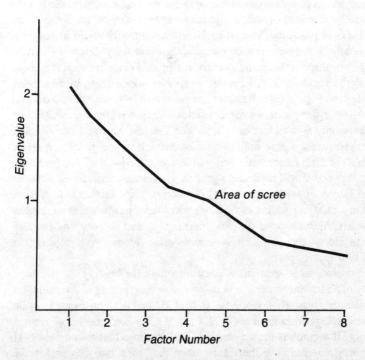

The scree is clearly visible in the data of Figure 8.3. However, most data produce no scree, so that other alternatives are needed. In fact the best guide to factor number is given by a conceptual analysis of the meanings of the factors extracted. Generally it is best to take as many factors as can reasonably be interpreted from an analysis of the pattern of item correlations for each factor. Thus factor I may be a general factor, factor II an age factor, factor III a bias factor, factor IV a potential sub-scale factor, and so on; eventually factors will be reached which are uninterpretable, and this is a good place to stop. An additional technique which is particularly useful can be used where there are large samples, and this is to break down the sample into sub-groups and investigate the extent of similarity between the separate factor analyses. The number of factors which look similar across populations is a good guide to a suitable factor number.

Factor rotation

The third set of options available in factor analysis programs deals with rotation. The idea of rotating factors has been around for some time, and was of particular interest to Thurstone in the 1930s. It arises only in situations where one factor is inadequate to fully describe the data and two, three or more factors are required. Factor rotation can most easily be explained within the visual representations model we have been using (see Figure 8.4); however, as we can only represent two dimensions on a flat paper we are restricted to representing the rotation of factors only two factors at a time. For the sake of simplicity we will consider a case where only two factors have been identified in a set of data. The first factor extracted will account for most of the variance, and the second will represent significant variance uncorrelated with the first factor. However, the actual position of these factors with respect to the underlying variables does not necessarily follow the arrangement that has the most psychological meaning. In fact there is any number of different ways in which we could define 'hidden' variables within the two factor space.

Consider as an example a situation where the loadings of five sub-tests of ability (arithmetic, calculation, science, reading and writing) on a factor analysis are 0.63, 0.54, 0.72, 0.81 and 0.45 on factor I, while their loadings on factor II are 0.72, 0.67. 0.45, −0.65 and −0.47 respectively. If a graph is drawn plotting these loadings on the two factors (I as the *y* axis and II as the *x* axis), then they form two clusters: in the top right-hand side we have mathematical abilities, while language abilities are in the top left-hand side of the graph. In this situation we could interpret factor I as a general ability factor, while factor II would contrast people who are good at mathematics and bad at language with people who are good at language and bad at mathematics. However, if we draw two new lines on this graph, both through the origin and at 45° to *x* and *y* respectively, we note that one of these lines passes through the mathematics cluster with no loadings on language, while the other passes through the language cluster with no loadings on mathematics. This could be interpreted as reflecting the existence of two independent ability factors, one of mathematics and one of language. Both these solutions are compatible with the same set of data! It can be seen that interpretation in factor analysis is never straightforward, and that to fully understand the results it is necessary to be fairly familiar with its underlying conception.

Figure 8.4 Rotation of orthogonal factors.

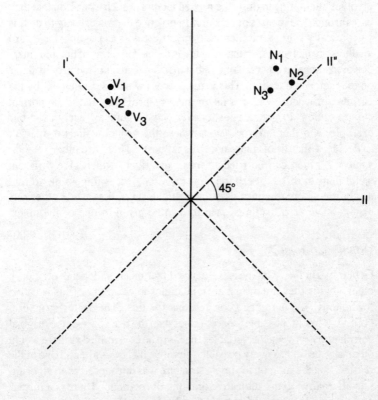

N1, N2, N3 are numerical sub-tests
V1, V2, V3, are language sub-tests
Factor loadings are plotted.

Rotation to simple structure

At one time, rotations of factor analytic data were carried out by hand, in the manner described above, and solutions sought by drawing lines on graphs which gave easily interpretable solutions. However, there was some criticism of this approach (although it is valid, merely open to abuse) on the grounds that it was too subjective. Thurstone therefore introduced a set of rules which specified standard procedures for rotation. The main one of these was 'rotation to simple structure'. The rotation carried out above on the mathematics and language data is such a rotation, and it involves attempting to draw the rotated factors in such a position that they pass through the major dot clusters. In practice the easiest way to do this algebraically is to require that as many of the dots as possible have zero loadings on the factors, so that rotation is defined in terms of the minimization of loadings on other factors, rather than of the maximization of loadings on the factor in question. This is the process which is carried out by the varimax procedure within a factor analysis program, and is the normal default option. In practice, data never behave quite as nicely as in our example, and there are occasions where the program finds it difficult to decide which fit of many poor fits is 'best'. There are other rotation solutions which can be tried in these situations, which give different weightings to different criteria. For example, if it is impossible to find a solution where the lines pass through one set of dots while other sets of dots have zero loadings, priority can be given to one or the other.

Orthogonal rotation

Generally, in factor analysis the derived factors are independent of each other, that is they are drawn at right angles to each other (this is called 'orthogonal'). There are good reasons for this. The factor structure, because it lies in 'possible' space, rather than the real space of the original correlations between the variables, needs to be constrained as there would otherwise be far too many possible solutions. This was after all one of the reasons that the rotation to simple structure was introduced as an algorithmic alternative to the subjective drawing of rotations. There is a further advantage of orthogonal factors in that they are relatively easy to interpret.

Oblique rotation

However, there are situations where the data do not sit happily about an orthogonal solution; and further situations were such a solution is artificial. It might be felt that there were good reasons why two particular factors would be expected to relate to each other. An example here might be sociability and impulsiveness as personality variables. In these situations there are procedures in most factor analytic programs for carrying out oblique solutions. These are more difficult to interpret as one of the main constraints has disappeared, and the factors found are not independent. The extent to which the orthogonality criteria can be relaxed can vary, and it is often found that different degrees of relaxation produce quite different solutions, so that a great deal of experience is required for rotations of this type. They are best avoided by people without experience of the technique.

Criticisms of the factor analytic approach

It is clear that factor analysis is a confusing technique that can easily produce contradictory results when used by the unwary. Generally, the analysis is particularly unsuited to testing hypotheses within the hypothetico-deductive model, as it can so easily be used to support almost any hypothesis from the same set of data. A common error is the assumption that if two variables have loadings on the same factor then they must be related. This is nonsense, as can be demonstrated by drawing two lines at right angles to each other, representing two uncorrelated variables, and then drawing a line between them at 45° to each, to represent a factor with 0.71 loading (the cosine of 45° is 0.71) from each variable! In early research major theoretical battles were often carried out on the basis of the results of different factor analytic rotations. For example, was there one factor of intelligence or many? These disputes were in the end seen as pure speculations; either position could be supported depending on how the data were interpreted. An important debate between Eysenck and Cattell about whether personality could be explained best in terms of two factors or sixteen turned out to be dependent on whether orthogonal or oblique rotations were used on the same data. Thus there could be two personality factors — or there could be sixteen, depending on how the situation was viewed.

A general dissatisfaction with factor analysis was widespread in the 1970s as a result of the apparent ability of the technique to fit almost any solution, and at this time strigent criteria were recommended concerning its use. In particular, it was felt that sample sizes had to be very large before the analysis was contemplated. In fact, the recommended samples were often so large as to render the use of factor analysis impractical. There were further constraints introduced in terms of the assumptions of the model, and in particular the requirement that the variables in the correlation matrix should have equivalent variance. This again produces a considerable practical problem as binary data in particular often fall short of this requirement, and item scores on psychometric tests are frequently binary.

Special uses of factor analysis in test construction

The reaction against factor analysis was carried to unreasonable extremes, which was unfortunate as it is a technique particularly suited to psychometrics. Much of the criticism has dealt with the inappropriateness of the factor analytic model within the hypothesis testing situation specified by the hypothetico-deductive model of science, where assumptions of normality and probability limit the interpretation of results. However, within item analysis, the constraints of the hypothetico-deductive model are not generally relevant unless hypotheses are actually being tested, and pragmatics often have a much larger say in whether items are selected. In the same way that item difficulties and item discriminations together with the test specification are used to make informed judgements, so can various solutions using factor analysis be informative about the number of sub-tests which are appropriate, the extent of guessing, the respondent's selection of socially desirable items, or the possibility of forms of cultural bias; and the use of factor analysis as a guide can be used to reduce any adverse effects. In real life situations where tests are being used, it is better to be guided by a set of factor analytic solutions, even if only based on relatively small numbers of respondents, than not to be so guided. Factor analysis is re-emerging as a pragmatic item analysis technique in the 1980s, and this has been helped in part by the development of log-linear models within factor analytic programs which are able to make adjustments for binary data.

The use of factor analysis for test construction is best seen in terms of validity. If we imagine the vector for the task and the vector for the test lying within the same factor space (as with the two vectors representing variables in Figure 8.2), then these will never in practice be perfectly identical. After all, validity is always a question of degree and thus we never expect perfect correlation between a test and its validation criterion. But the various different directions in which the test vector slants away from the task vector represent different possible forms of invalidity, and while the task vector itself will never appear within the factor analytic space, there will be vectors representing forms of contamination. Consider, for example, a factor analytic solution of the item correlation matrix for a test in which all positively worded items load on one factor and all negatively worded items on another (a not uncommon situation in practice). It is fairly evident if this happens that each of these factors has been contaminated by the acquiescence artifact. This occurs when some respondents have a tendency to agree with all the statements whatever their content, while others tend to disagree with all the statements. To put the matter simply, some people tend to say yes to everything, while others tend to say no to everything, causing all the items to correlate positively with each other, regardless of content. If, however, we plot both of these factors on a piece of graph paper we will almost certainly be able to identify a rotation which gives the underlying test scale and the acquiescence effect as separate factors (probably not orthogonal). We can then use this graph in addition to our other item analysis data to choose items which effectively cancel out any acquiescence effect, an option which would not have been possible without the factor analytic technique.

Another effective use of factor analysis in test construction is in the reduction of confabulation (the lying effect). By introducing a few lie items into the pilot study (such as the 'I have never stolen anything in my life, not even a pin' within the Eysenck Personality Inventory), we can obtain a factor which represents lying, and we can again choose items which rotate the prime test vector away from a contamination with this unwanted effect.

A further major use of factor analysis within test construction is for testing the adequacy of the unidimensional model. As discussed earlier, it is normally the purpose of a test that is important in determining whether a unidimensional single score or a multidimensional sub-score structure is required. However, there may well be situations, usually as a result of ambiguities within the test specification or of a large number of unreliable or invalid items, where a simple unidimensional scale actually seems to misrepresent the data. Factor analysis will make this explicit and offer guidance for any decisions of principle which need to be made, such as whether to proceed with the attempt to construct a single scale and, if not, what the alternatives are. In other situations factor analysis can be used to explore the feasibility of a sub-scale structure for a domain which is reasonably secure and has been well explored. Such sub-scale structures can be particularly informative for further diagnosis, and are in wide use in profiles, such as the Minnesota Multiphasic Personality Inventory (MMPI) (Hathaway and McKinley 1965), or the Golombok Rust Inventory of Sexual Satisfaction (GRISS) (Rust and Golombok 1985, 1986a, 1986b). As sub-scales normally correlate with each other, their inter-relations need to be known, otherwise conflicting interpretations would ensue. This is particularly true in the Cattell personality scales such as the 16PF (Cattell 1965), where sub-scales often have inter-correlations as high as 0.7. In these circumstances it is almost certain that if a respondent has a high score on one sub-scale then several other sub-scale scores will be high as well, with a consequent danger of over-interpretation. Factor analysis can also be used to ensure that sub-scales used are reasonably stable across different populations and different circumstances. Factor analysis of all the test items under different circumstances is particularly useful for deciding whether separate sub-scales are required, and whether they are valid. When used with caution, with insight and with pragmatism, factor analysis is an invaluable tool in test construction, although sometimes a dangerous one.

Summary

The procedures of factor analysis were developed very early in the history of psychometrics, and provide a useful way for workers in the area to make visual representations of the scales they are using. Although the technique is open to abuse it can, if used properly, be a considerable aid to test construction and be very informative about the underlying structure of a set of scores.

Chapter nine

Psychometrics in the information technology age

Psychometric procedures have proved to be particularly amenable to computerization, so much so that the growth of these techniques is now a threat to many human traditions. The fact that tests usually contain information about an individual's psychological make-up, that they are normally scored by computer, that once scored the data can easily be transferred to data banks, and that data of this type are always of interest to personnel and credit agencies, social security, the police and intelligence services, does mean that special care needs to be taken, especially now that large data banks are able to extract information in 'intelligent' ways. The contribution of computers to testing for college entrance, professional licensure tests, standardized achievement batteries and scored clinical instruments is enormous, although not immediately apparent to the large number of people who are affected by it. Computerization of scoring, of test design, and of reliability and validity estimation is leading to significant improvements in the dependability of testing, and this is proceeding at an ever increasing rate.

Computerized statistics

The impact of the computer has taken place at several levels. The first major development was of the computerized statistical package, first on mainframe computers and now on micros. Most problems in psychometrics are extensions of matrix algebra and it has been this area of mathematics which has been most influenced. Before the 1940s, the main restrictions on psychometrics were time limitations based on the need to carry out large numbers of calculations. In factor analysis in particular, matrix inversion is essential but time consuming. Further, because iteration is required for the solution of many multi-linear equations, each major algorithm needed to be carried out several times. After the 1950s computers became essential for these types of problem, which were able to be tackled in full for the first time. However, many hours of computer time were still needed. By the 1980s factor analysis programs were available on microcomputers, and by the 1990s even complex modelling will be easily available to every personal computer owner.

One difficulty that has been found generally with the ready availability of statistical packages is that obtaining the solution to the computational problem has outrun actual understanding of the psychological problem. Thus many inexperienced users find that the computers can produce almost endless alternative ways of analysis, different forms of significance test, and rotations of factor structure, but very little guidance on what is actually important out of all these many pages of figures. The use of knowledge engineering techniques will certainly change this situation, and by the early 1990s we can expect to find programs available which can carry out for us all the important steps in the analysis of results from a pilot study, that can tell us what form of factor structure is most appropriate, and advise on the selection or alteration of items for the new version of the test.

Computerized item banks

The next most important area in which computerization is having an impact is in the development and administration of item banks (see Chapter 4). The development of item response theory (IRT), and in particular of item characteristic models of item bank structure, enables a great deal of housekeeping of the bank to be done automatically. Item characteristic curve models involve complex iteration, and during the 1970s analysis of the two and three parameter models was too expensive in computer time, so that item banks were almost exclusively based on the Rasch one parameter model. This was known to be inadequate in any controversial setting. However, by the 1980s the more complex models were no longer such a challenge, and were beginning to become widely available (Bock and Mislevy 1982). The IRT models enable the responses from the early items in a test to be used to give a provisional estimate of ability and use this to present a more specific set of items for the rest of the test matched to this estimated ability (Haladyna and Roid 1983). These methods when fully developed will save up to 50% on the number of items required, and can thus either save time or increase precision. The use of this technique in personality and attitude testing is discussed by Wright and Masters (1982), while Hambleton and Swaminathan (1985) have carried out an empirical study to show that sequential adaptive tests of this type can provide greater precision and reliability with fewer items than conventional achievement tests.

One important example of the use of IRT models in test construction is the British Ability Scale. For a long time in the late 1970s, at a time when the Rasch model had fallen into disfavour, it was felt that the use of item theory in the construction of this scale had been a mistake. However, the test itself proved to have been so well constructed overall, and so useful in practice, that the use of the Rasch constructed sub-scales of numerical and other computational abilities was recommended albeit with caution. In fact, they have proved to be particularly robust in their use for the clinical assessment of children, and the generalization across ability levels from different sub-sets of items has, in spite of many misgivings, been found to be informative. Elliot (1983) argues that many of the misgivings about the Rasch model have arisen from situations where it has been applied to pre-existing data, or to test data which had not been specifically designed to fit the model. If the Rash model is used carefully and with a full knowledge of its limitations, as in the development of the British Ability Scale, then it is possible to make use of its subject free and item free characteristics.

Computerized item generation

A further addition to the repertoire of item bank management programs by the 1990s will be the ability to tailor, alter and even create new items. The use of computers in the construction of test items goes back to the work of Atkinson and Wilson (1969), who constructed a series of small computer program sections (macros) that allowed for individual test-like events in instruction, such as checking whether recently presented material had been learned, to be varied at will. These were incorporated within a computer assisted learning (CAL) program, and this pattern of instructional material leading to a test and then the presentation of more material, forms the backbone of many CAL programs in use today. The utility of the computer in designing test items is based largely on the existence of a series of standard formats in items. Thus many items have a frame, which is held constant, and elements, which can vary. Take the object relations format, a is to b as x is to y. Possible insertions here are, for example, glove is to hand as sock is to ? (foot), but there are many millions of possible sets of semantic relations which could participate in an item of this type. The same is true for most item types, and indeed item types themselves are severely limited in number; it is the enormous number of possible elements which provides for variation. There are many circumstances where sets of possible elements can be held in store and inserted by computer at random into a fixed format to generate a large series of new items. This applies particularly in memory tests but also in perceptual and numeric tests. In fact the possibility for a degree of computerization exists in almost every type of test item. The advantages of this are several but particularly lie in the ability to create new items at will in circumstances where subjects need to be tested several times.

Computerized test administration

The overlap between psychometrics and curriculum implementation is in many ways at its most explicit within computer assisted learning (CAL), and this usefully illustrates both the limitations and strengths of the psychometric model. The CAL model normally involves the sitting of the pupil in front of a computer screen, following which a program will be initiated which presents information on the screen and asks the pupil questions about the material. A CAL program needs to be able to utilize the responses of the pupil to identify his or her learning needs, to present material which will stimulate learning, and to form some assessment of its (and the pupil's) success or failure. Within CAL the main aim is towards the learning of the subject, and the test items within a CAL program are subsidiary; they exist to identify very specific, and hopefully temporary, blocks in understanding, and to diagnose the best way forward. They mirror the type of dialogue which might occur between a teacher and a student, and can be considered as teacher 'expert systems'.

Computerized questioning

The common characteristics of CAL and computerized psychometrics might seem to imply that they are really the same process and only differ as a matter of degree. However, this is probably misleading. Psychometric computerized test administration differs from CAL in that the questions are intended to identify long-term characteristics of the respondent. The test items thus need to be more carefully constructed and piloted. This is in fact true even within educational settings involving continuous assessment. While there is no clear dividing line between the immediate demands of CAL based questioning and the longer term psychometric items, it is normally considered the case that psychometrics as such only begins where written reports are made. Thus if a differentiation is needed between CAL question items and psychometric question items within computerized testing, it is that between the immediate response which goes towards initiating the next step in a CAL program, and the stored response which makes a concrete contribution to whatever records are taken away afterwards from the session. With the latter there is clearly the expectation that what has happened during the session has implications for subsequent action, and indeed can be relied on to predict subsequent action. The subsequent use of test scores for judging the child, teacher or school is normally justified in terms of psychological or educational theory. Within education, it will be defined around steps in the curriculum process, in psychology around theoretical constructs.

Automated reporting

A further way in which the use of the computer is being extended is in the generation of reports. Many tests no longer report mere numbers, to be interpreted by experts, but are able to give information directly to an end user. Where the test is a profile battery, the computer is able to identify extremes, to interpret these in the light of other sub-scale scores, and to make recommendations. This extension of use also implies an extension of the validation process from end score to end interpretation. However, it does mean that a much more rigid series of justification rules needs to be made for recommendations made on the basis of test scores generated by computer. Consider the similar case of computerized medical diagnosis. If, within this procedure, an error is made, the wrong medication prescribed and the patient dies as a result, who is accountable for this mistake? Is it the computer, the clinician, or the person who wrote the diagnostic program? When diagnosis was carried out by the clinical expert alone there was at least a clear knowledge of who was accountable in the event of error. As computers obviously cannot be held accountable in law, the use of computer recommendations might appear to pass the responsibility to the test constructor; however, it is more likely the end user who will be left with de facto responsibility. This implies that in future, computer programs which make recommendations should also be programmed to justify their decision rules. It should never be the case that a person is in the position where he or she can say, 'This is the computer's decision'. This meaning-less statement can only be eradicated if the advisors are taken by the computer through the steps required to back up the decision, so that the computer can fulfil its proper role as an aid to decision making.

The ethical issues associated with computerized advice of this type are reviewed by Zachary and Pope (1983). Roid (1986) points out that there are four major concerns which arise from the use of computers in test interpretation: (i) that it is questionable whether computers are any better than human experts, (ii) that the computerized reports may reach the hands of inexperienced or unqualified people, (iii) that the deci-sion rules may not be public, and (iv) that computerized reports may not be sufficiently validated. Many of these arguments are directed towards 'expert' computer systems in general, and although they all include an element of truth, it seems unreasonable at this stage of develop-ment to argue for abolition. As with expert systems in general, the prob-lems both ethical and social which they present to society will have to be tackled one way or another, for better or worse. A code of conduct will almost certainly be required which specifies where records are kept, who shall have access, the purposes for which they shall be used, the validation techniques and procedures for making public the decision rules. The problems are similar to those encountered in the use of computerized expert systems for any decision making process involving human beings, where thought has to be given to the consequences of a wrong decision which may have to be justified in a court of law.

Automated recommendations and issues of responsibility

These ethical issues might also apply wherever psychometric tests are combined with actuarial prediction procedures. McDermott (1980) developed a program which was able to identify students in a variety of special education categories based on scores on the Wechsler Intelligence Scale for Children (revised edition) (WISC-R), the revised version of the Wide Range Achievement Test (WRAT-R), the Adaptive Behaviour Scales and several other tests. On the basis of these scores the program would print out probability estimates for each category. This technique could be carried out by hand, and therefore has no new pit-falls which are not already covered by legislation on the use of these tests individually. However, a program by Barclay (1983), the Barclay Classroom Assessment System, provides an example of a computerized battery which was so extensive in scope and complexity that the procedures, involving sociometric choices by each member of each classroom among all other members, could not be realistically replicated without the program. The value of the computer in these circumstances is that it makes possible an analysis which would be otherwise impossible, but this is at the expense of a diminution in clarity about the lines of responsibility. Actuarial programs have also been developed for use with the Minnesota Multiphasic Personality Inventory (MMPI), and studies comparing these programs with human experts have generally given them a good success rate (Lachar 1974).

Computerized scoring

While computers have been used for scoring tests for some time, some developments have taken place recently which are likely to revolutionize this process. The most important and straightforward is the use of scanners for reading response sheets, a development which makes the objective test an even more attractive option for selection bodies dealing with many applications or for education authorities attempting to sample whole school populations. As computers increase the ease with which data from large numbers of individuals can be processed, more precise forms of norming become possible. In the past many developmental tests have suffered from a lack of precision in age groupings, based on the need for large samples. For a developmental test to be valid it is necessary to have fairly large normative samples at every age. Even annual sampling is not sufficiently precise, so that groupings every six months are required. But even here, large differences can be found between the standardized score of an individual who was at the oldest limit of a category, say one day under six and a half years, and the standardized score received if the child had been two days older and at the bottom of the next category. This problem becomes more severe the more precise the test. Zachary and Gorsuch (1985) have put forward a computerized procedure for continuous norming of norm referenced tests, such that the program is able to take into account the actual ages (to the day) of all children in the standardization sample to generate a curve fitting procedure to give a more accurate estimate of the child's score in relation to his or her peers. In this technique, values of test means and standard deviations are effectively 'smoothed' across age groups so that estimates can be made for any age.

Computerized administration

Computerized administration of tests has been used for some time, with several advantages over individually administered or paper and pencil tests. Individual test administration in particular is a time consuming yet fairly automatic process for many tests, so that computerization offers potential savings in professional time. Klinger, Johnson, and Williams (1976) have shown that when used in clinical settings there is also an increased acceptance by patients. It seems that often people are happier to answer questions for a computer than they are for their fellow human beings! However, the mere placing of a test on a computer for easier administration is only the first step in the utilization of computers for test administration. Because of their speed and infallible memory computer programs can easily be written which allow the computer to adapt its questioning to the initial responses of the subject. In a paper and pencil test we have no way of knowing how a subject will respond, so that all eventualities have to be covered. With a computerized adaptive test, on the other hand, any questions which turn out to be irrelevant after some initial information is known can be eliminated. It is also possible to tailor the difficulty level of a test to the ability level of an applicant. If the subject encounters difficulty, the test can be made progressively easier, and if the subject finds the test too easy it can be made more difficult. This procedure tends to increase the motivation of the subject in either case. It is further possible to target special areas of the blueprint and allow the program to select questions which focus in on a particular area. Thus if we are interested in whether a person scores above a particular cut-off on a test it is possible to use a Bayesian approach which always chooses as the next item one which will maximize information towards making a decision, and to stop as soon as a specified probability level of acceptance or rejection is reached. Adaptive testing seems such an obvious way forward that it is surprising that it has not become more widely used. There are several studies which have shown it to be more successful than classical techniques for both criterion referenced (Haladyna and Roid 1983) and norm referenced tests (Hambleton and Swaminathan 1985). Reasons for the technique not becoming universally popular may include the lack of software, the sophistication needed to interpret the item response theory models involved, and the lack of faith of educational and psychological professionals in models they cannot understand.

Computerized 'expert systems'

The information technology revolution, in addition to changing the methods of psychometrics, can also produce new models of the activity of psychometricians by modelling their various activities within computerized expert systems. In many ways the procedures involved in any use of a test, whether evaluative, diagnostic or selective, are standard procedures involving the expertise of professional psychologists, personnel managers, clinicians and educators. Expert system design has several stages, the first of which is to elicit the information from the experts themselves. This is done by interviewing, by observing the experts actually working on problems, and by a variety of psychological techniques such as semantic differentials, sociometry, etc. As much expert knowledge is claimed to be more or less intuitive by the experts themselves, the elicitation of these types of expert knowledge can be very illuminating, and many of the observed decision making processes, when made explicit, come as a surprise to the experts themselves. Thus when expert system technology is applied to the activity of psychometricians the procedures produced tend to exemplify, refine and make explicit the underlying psychometric theory.

Rather paradoxically, the models produced by this approach are more similar to those of realist psychometrics in that they use the expert's conceptions of intervening personality and aptitude traits, rather than the pure functional behaviour expected under the functional model. It seems to be the case that even psychometricians who are wedded to the functional approach in practice make use of trait based ideas about personality in deciding which functions are relevant. This paradox is yet another exemplifier of a common theme we have come across time and time again throughout this book. The functional approach to psychometrics only works when we are able to summarize and classify the various functions of the test. And to do this we need psychological traits to structure our psychological knowledge. In principle a computer would seem to be ideally suited, through its powerful number crunching ability with enormous numbers of variables, to the application of functional analysis in selecting a person for a job. If this is to be done functionally there will be an enormous number of factors involved in identifying the right person, and all of these behaviours must interact in complex ways. One consequence of using a computer in this manner, however, will be that human beings, because they cannot deal with large numbers of variables in the same way, can not have a full picture of the actual information and procedures involved in a particular decision. Such a manner of utilizing computers, therefore, although often actuarially the most correct, is not likely to receive widespread acceptance as it would be impossible for a human being to give a straightforward account of how the decision was made. Certainly in the immediate future, the computer is likely to be used as an assistant rather than an alternative to human judgment. All steps involved in any computer guided decision will need to be understandable and clearly stated if the human expert is to be accountable for any recommendations made. Societal forces in the end will probably demand that computers become human, rather than accept the decisions of actuarial number crunching machines.

Summary

Information technology is having a revolutionary impact on psychometrics. The first stage was the application of the number crunching power of mainframe computers to the necessary statistical calculations of item analysis, reliability estimation and more general experimental design. More recently the computer has been able to take over the role of test administration, and here, because the machine is able to make decisions so quickly, a new stage of development has been reached where results obtained at the beginning of a testing session can be analysed in time to modify the progress of the session. In the immediate future there is also additional promise from the application of expert systems technology to psychometrics. The potential for computers to model decision processes at a linguistic as well as an information processing level promises to be one of the most productive and controversial areas of development in not just psychometrics but in social decision making generally.

Part two

Chapter ten

Constructing your own questionnaire

Questionnaires are often no more than a series of items which are not necessarily related to each other and which are scored and interpreted individually. This is a guide to the construction of psychometric questionnaires, i.e. where items can be combined to produce an overall scale.

Questionnaires are used to measure a wide variety of attributes and characteristics. The most common examples are knowledge based questionnaires, i.e. questionnaires of ability, aptitude and achievement; and person based questionnaires, i.e. questionnaires of personality, clinical symptoms, mood and attitudes. Whatever type of questionnaire you wish to develop, this guide will take you through the main stages of construction and will also show you how to tailor your questionnaire to its particular purpose. Throughout the guide the construction of the Golombok Rust Inventory of Marital State (GRIMS) (Rust et al. 1988) will be described (in italics) as a practical example.

The purpose of the questionnaire

The first step in developing a questionnaire is to ask yourself 'What is it for?' Unless you have a clear and precise answer to this question your questionnaire will not tell you what you want to know.

With the GRIMS we wanted to develop a questionnaire TO ASSESS THE QUALITY OF THE RELATIONSHIP IN HETEROSEXUAL COUPLES WHO ARE MARRIED OR LIVING TOGETHER. We intended that the GRIMS would be of use in research, either to help therapists or counsellors to evaluate the effectiveness of therapy for couples with relationship problems, or to investigate the impact of social, psychological, medical or other factors on a relationship. In addition, we hoped that it would be used clinically as a quick and easy to administer technique for identifying the severity of a problem, for finding out which partner perceives a problem in the relationship, and for identifying any improvement or lack of improvement in either or both partners over time.

WRITE DOWN CLEARLY AND PRECISELY THE PURPOSE OF YOUR QUESTIONNAIRE.

Making a blueprint

A blueprint, sometimes known as the test specification, is a framework for developing the questionnaire. A grid structure is generally used with (a) CONTENT AREAS along the horizontal axis and (b) MANIFESTA- TIONS (ways in which the content areas may become manifest) along the vertical axis. For practical reasons, between 4 and 7 categories are usually employed along each axis. Fewer often results in too narrow a questionnaire, and more can be too cumbersome to deal with.

CONTENT AREAS

MANIFESTATIONS

(A) CONTENT AREAS A clear purpose will enable you to specify the content of your questionnaire. The content areas should cover everything that is relevant to the purpose of the questionnaire.

The many different ideas about what constitutes a good or bad marriage posed a problem when trying to specify the content areas of the GRIMS. For this reason we used the expertise of marital therapists/counsellors and their clients. The therapists/counsellors were asked to identify areas which they believed to be important in marital harmony as well as the areas they would assess during initial interviews. Information from clients was obtained by asking them to identify their targets for change. The views of these experts were collated to provide the following content areas which were generally considered to be important for assessing the state of a relationship:

(i) interests shared (work, politics, friends, etc.) and degree of dependence and independence (ii) communication (verbal and non-verbal) (iii) sex (iv) warmth, love and hostility (v) trust and respect (vi) roles, expectations and goals (vii) decision making (viii) coping with problems and crises.

WRITE DOWN THE CONTENT AREAS TO BE COVERED BY YOUR QUESTIONNAIRE. IF THESE ARE NOT CLEAR-CUT, CONSULT EXPERTS IN THE FIELD.

(B) MANIFESTATIONS The ways in which the content areas may manifest themselves will vary according to the type of questionnaire under construction. For example, questionnaires designed to measure educational attainment may use Bloom's taxonomy of educational objectives to tap different forms of knowledge. For questionnaires which are more psychological in nature, behavioural, cognitive and affective manifestations of the content areas may be more appropriate. In specifying manifestations it is important to ensure that different aspects of the content areas will be elicited.

In constructing the GRIMS we again took account of the experts' information to obtain the following manifestations: (i) beliefs about, insight into and understanding of the nature of dyadic relationships (ii) behaviour within the actual relationship (ii) attitudes and feelings about relationships (iv) motivation for change, understanding the possibility of change, and commitment to a future together (v) extent of agreement within the couple.

As you can see from the GRIMS blueprint, what is described as a content area and what is described as a manifestation may not always be clear cut.

WRITE DOWN WAYS IN WHICH THE CONTENT AREAS OF YOUR QUESTIONNAIRE MAY BECOME MANIFEST.

You will now be able to construct your blueprint. The number of cells will be the number of content areas × the number of manifestations. Between 16 and 25 cells (i.e. 4 × 4, 4 × 5, 5 × 4 or 5 × 5) are generally considered ideal for sufficient breadth while maintaining manageability.

DRAW YOUR BLUEPRINT, LABELLING EACH CONTENT AREA (COLUMNS) AND EACH MANIFESTATION (ROWS).

Each cell in the blueprint represents the interaction of a content area with a manifestation of that content area. By writing items for your questionnaire which correspond to each cell of the blueprint, you will ensure that all aspects which are relevant to the purpose of your questionnaire will be covered.

A decision which has to be made when designing the blueprint is whether to give different weightings to each of the cells, i.e. whether to write more items for some cells than for others. This will depend on whether or not you feel that some content areas or some manifestations are more important than others. In the blueprint below it has been decided that content area A should receive a weighting of 40%, content area B a weighting of 40%, content area C a weighting of 10% and content area D a weighting of 10%. For the manifestations, a weighting of 25% has been allocated to each.

Content areas

		A 40%	B 40%	C 10%	D 10%
Manifestations	A 25%				
	B 25%				
	C 25%				
	D 25%				

For the GRIMS, equal weightings were assigned to each cell as we had no reason to believe that any of the content areas or manifestations were more important than the others.

ASSIGN PERCENTAGES TO EACH CONTENT AREA OF YOUR BLUEPRINT SO THAT THE TOTAL OF THE PERCENTAGES ACROSS THE CONTENT AREAS ADDS UP TO 100%.

ASSIGN PERCENTAGES TO EACH MANIFESTATION IN YOUR BLUEPRINT SO THAT THE TOTAL OF THE PERCENTAGES ACROSS THE MANIFESTATIONS ADDS UP TO 100%.

INSERT THESE PERCENTAGES INTO YOUR BLUEPRINT.

Assigning weightings will tell you what proportion of all items in the questionnaire should be written for each cell. The next step is to decide upon the total number of items to include. You must consider factors such as the size of your blueprint (a large blueprint with many content areas and manifestations will need a greater number of items than a small one) and the amount of time available for administering the questionnaire. There is no point in asking people with little time to spare to complete a lengthy inventory, as the quality of their response will be poor and items may be omitted. Characteristics of the respondents are also important. The elderly and the physically ill may be slow and unable to maintain concentration. Although it is important to include a sufficient number of items to ensure high reliability, compliance among respondents is crucial and a balance must be struck between the two. A minimum of 20 items is usually required to achieve good reliability, and a fairly straightforward questionnaire of this length should take the average respondent no longer than ten minutes to complete. As it is necessary to construct a pilot version of your questionnaire in the first instance, you must remember to allow for at least 50% more items in the blueprint than you intend to include in the final version.

The GRIMS was intended as a short questionnaire for use with both distressed and non-distressed couples. As we hoped to achieve a final scale of about 30 items, we planned a pilot version with 100 items.

DECIDE HOW MANY ITEMS TO INCLUDE IN THE PILOT VERSION OF YOUR QUESTIONNAIRE BY TAKING INTO ACCOUNT THE DESIRED NUMBER OF ITEMS IN THE FINAL VERSION, THE SIZE OF YOUR BLUEPRINT, THE TIME AVAILABLE FOR TESTING AND THE CHARACTERISTICS OF THE RESPONDENTS.

Once you have assigned weightings to the cells and decided upon the total number of items you require for your pilot questionnaire, you will be able to work out how many items to write for each cell. The blueprint below, with given weightings, shows the number of items which have to be written for each cell to obtain a pilot questionnaire with 80 items. The first step is to work out the total number of items for each content area and for each manifestation. The blueprint specifies that 40% of the items (32 items) should be on content area A, 40% on content area B (32 items), 10% (8 items) on content area C and 10% (8 items) on content area D. These numbers are entered in the bottom row of the blueprint. Similarly, the blueprint specifies that 25% of the items (20 items) should concern each of the manifestations and this is entered into the right-hand column of the blueprint. To calculate the number of items in each cell

of the blueprint, multiply the *total* number of items in a content area
by the percentage assigned to the manifestation in each row. For example,
the number of items for the top left-hand cell (content area A/manifesta-
tion A) is 25% of 32 items, which is 8 items. The number of items to
be written for each cell is calculated in the same way. If you do not obtain
an exact number of items for a cell, approximate to the number above
or below while trying to maintain the same total number of items as you
had originally planned.

	Content areas				
	A 40%	B 40%	C 10%	D 10%	No. of items
A 25%	8	8	2	2	20
B 25%	8	8	2	2	20
C 25%	8	8	2	2	20
D 25%	8	8	2	2	20
No. of items	32	32	8	8	80

Manifestations

*The 100 items in the equally weighted 40 cell GRIMS blueprint
allowed between 2 and 4 items per cell.*

ENTER THE NUMBER OF ITEMS TO BE WRITTEN FOR EACH
CELL INTO YOUR BLUEPRINT.

Writing items

There are several types of items which are used in questionnaires, the
most common of which are ALTERNATE CHOICE items, MULTIPLE
CHOICE items and RATING SCALE items. Different item types are
suitable for different purposes and consideration of the attribute or
characteristic which you wish your questionnaire to measure will guide
you towards an appropriate choice.

TYPE   ALTERNATE CHOICE ITEM. An item
for which the respondent is given two
choices from which to select a response, e.g.
'true' or 'false', 'yes' or 'no'.

USE	Most commonly used in knowledge based questionnaires. E.g. Bogota is the capital of Colombia — true or false?
	Sometimes used in personality questionnaires. E.g. I never use a lucky charm — yes or no?
	Generally considered inappropriate for clinical symptoms, mood or attitude questionnaires but used occasionally.
ADVANTAGES	Good for assessing knowledge of facts and comprehension of material presented in the question. Fast and easy to use.
DISADVANTAGES	For ability, aptitude and achievement items, the correct response is often not clear cut, i.e. completely true or completely false. Another problem is that the respondent has a 50% chance of obtaining the correct response by guessing. For personality, clinical symptoms, mood and attitude questionnaires, there are no right or wrong answers. However, respondents often consider the narrow range of possible responses to be too restricting.
TYPE	MULTIPLE CHOICE ITEM. An item for which the respondent is given more than two choices from which to select a response. It consists of two parts: (i) the stem — a statement or question which contains the problem and (ii) the options — a list of possible responses of which one is correct or best and the others are distractors. Often 4 or 5 possible responses are used to reduce the probability of guessing the answer.
USE	Most widely used item type in knowledge based questionnaires. E.g. What is the capital of Colombia? A. La Paz

B. Bogota

C. Lima

D. Santiago

Not used in person based questionnaires.

ADVANTAGES

Well suited to the wide variety of material which may be presented in ability, aptitude and achievement questionnaires. Challenging items can be constructed which are easy to administer and score. The effects of guessing are also reduced with multiple choice items. For example, an item with 5 options gives a 20% chance of guessing the correct answer compared with 50% in alternate response items.

DISADVANTAGES

Time and skill are needed for writing good multiple choice items. A common problem is that not all of the options are effective, i.e. that they are so unlikely to be correct that they do not function as possible options. This can reduce what is intended as a 5 choice item to a 3 or 4 choice item or even to an alternate choice item.

TYPE

RATING SCALE ITEM. An item for which the possible responses lie along a continuum, e.g. 'yes', 'don't know', 'no'; 'true', 'uncertain', 'false'; 'strongly disagree', 'disagree', 'agree', 'strongly agree'; 'always', 'sometimes', 'occasionally', 'hardly ever', 'never'. Up to 7 options are generally used as it is difficult for respondents to differentiate meaningfully among more than that number. Although rating scale items are similar to multiple choice items in giving several response options, the options in rating scales are interdependent while multiple choice item options are independent of each other.

USE

Not used in knowledge based questionnaires.

Most widely used item type in person based questionnaires. E.g. I am not a superstitious person

A. strongly disagree
B. disagree
C. agree
D. strongly agree

ADVANTAGES | Respondents feel able to express themselves more precisely with rating scale items than with alternate choice items.

DISADVANTAGES | Respondents differ in their interpretations of the response options, e.g. 'frequently' has a different meaning to different individuals. Some respondents tend always to choose the most extreme options. When an uneven number of response options is used, many respondents tend to choose the middle one, e.g. 'don't know', or 'occasionally'.

The TYPE OF OPTION should be chosen to suit the material to be presented in the questionnaire. There are no fixed rules about which type of option is best. A personality or mood questionnaire might require responses in terms of the options 'not at all', 'somewhat' and very much'. Attitude questionnaires generally consist of statements about an attitude object followed by the options 'strongly agree', 'agree', 'uncertain', 'disagree' or 'strongly disagree'. For clinical symptoms questionnaires, you might find that options relating to the frequency of occurrence, such as 'always', 'sometimes', 'occasionally', 'hardly ever' or 'never', are the most suitable.

The most appropriate NUMBER OF OPTIONS to choose will also depend on the nature of the questionnaire. It is important to provide a sufficient number for respondents to feel able to express themselves adequately while ensuring that there are not so many that they have to make meaningless discriminations. In questionnaires using rating scale items where strength of response should be reflected in the respondent's score, it is usual for at least 4 options to be used.

It is sometimes necessary to use different types of item in a questionnaire because of the nature of the material to be included. However, it is preferable to use only one item type wherever possible to produce a neatly presented questionnaire.

> *Rating Scale items are the most appropriate for a scale of marital state. The items are presented as statements to which the respondents are asked to 'strongly agree', 'agree', 'disagree' or 'strongly disagree'. This spread of options allows strength of feeling to affect scores. The items are forced choice, i.e. there is no 'don't know' category.*

DECIDE WHICH ITEM TYPE IS MOST APPROPRIATE FOR YOUR QUESTIONNAIRE. IN GENERAL, MULTIPLE CHOICE ITEMS ARE BEST FOR KNOWLEDGE BASED QUESTIONNAIRES, AND RATING SCALE ITEMS ARE BEST FOR PERSON BASED QUES-TIONNAIRES UNLESS YOU HAVE GOOD REASON, SUCH AS SPEED OR SIMPLICITY, FOR CHOOSING ALTERNATE CHOICE ITEMS. A GOOD METHOD FOR DECIDING WHICH TO CHOOSE IS TO TRY TO CONSTRUCT ITEMS OF EACH TYPE USING DIFFERENT OPTIONS. THE MOST APPROPRIATE CHOICE FOR YOUR QUESTIONNAIRE WILL SOON BECOME CLEAR.

Before beginning to write items for your questionnaire, read the following summary of important points to remember. For a more detailed discussion of how to write good items see Thorndike and Hagen (1977) and Guilford (1959).

All questionnaires

Make sure that your items match your blueprint. The allocation of items to specific cells may become a bit fuzzy as some items may be appropriate for more than one cell. If you find that some cells are inappropriate and you decide to omit them, do not do so without proper consideration. Remember, however, that the blueprint is a guide and not a straightjacket.

Write each item clearly and simply. Avoid irrelevant material and keep the options as short as possible. Each item should ask only one question or make only one statement. Where possible, avoid subjective words such as 'frequently', as these may be interpreted differently by different respondents. It is also important that all options are functioning as feasible responses, i.e. that none is clearly wrong or irrelevant and, therefore, unlikely to be chosen.

After writing your items, read them again a few days later. Also ask a colleague to look at them to ensure that they are easily understood and unambiguous.

Knowledge based questionnaires

Make sure that alternate choice items can be classified without doubt as true or false, otherwise some respondents will think of exceptions to the rule.

For multiple choice items, ensure that each item has only one correct or best response. Ideally, each distractor option should be used equally by respondents who do not choose the correct response. Remember that the more similar the options, the more difficult the item.

Person based questionnaires

Sometimes respondents will complete a questionnaire in a certain way irrespective of the content of the items:

AQUIESCENCE is the tendency to agree with items regardless of their content. This can be reduced by ensuring that an equal or almost equal number of items is scored in each direction. To do this, it is usually necessary to reverse some of the items. For example, the item 'I am satisfied with our relationship' can be reversed to 'I am dissatisfied with our relationship'. When reversing items it is important to check that the reversed item has the same meaning as the original item. It is best to avoid double negative statements as these cause confusion. Aquiescence is less likely to occur with items which are clear, unambiguous and specific.

SOCIAL DESIRABILITY is the tendency to respond to an item in a socially acceptable manner. This can be reduced by excluding items which are clearly socially desirable or undesirable. If this is unavoidable due to the nature of your questionnaire, try to ask the question indirectly to evoke a response which is not simply a reflection of how the respondent wishes to present him or herself. For example, an item to measure paranoia may be subtly phrased as 'there are some people whom I trust completely' rather than 'people are plotting against me'. Social desirability can also be reduced by asking respondents to give an immediate response rather than a careful consideration of each item.

INDECISIVENESS is the tendency to use the 'don't know' or 'uncertain' option. This is a common problem which can easily be eliminated by omitting the middle category. It is advisable to do so unless respondents are likely to become irritated by items which they feel are unanswerable.

EXTREME RESPONSE is the tendency to choose an extreme option regardless of direction. Some respondents will use one direction for a series of items and then switch to the other direction and so on. Again, this can be reduced by the use of clear, unambiguous and specific items.

It is important to bear in mind these habitual ways of responding when writing items. However, a careful item analysis will eliminate items which are biased towards a particular response.

Examples of GRIMS items:
'We both seem to like the same things' was written for the blueprint cell representing content area (i) and manifestation (ii).
'I wish there was more warmth and affection between us' was written for the blueprint cell representing content area (iv) and manifestation (iv).

WRITE EACH OF YOUR ITEMS ON A SMALL CARD SO THAT YOU CAN EASILY MAKE CHANGES IN WORDING AND ORDERING. TO ORDER THE ITEMS FOR YOUR QUESTIONNAIRE PICK AN INTERESTING AND UNTHREATENING ITEM TO START WITH AND THEN SHUFFLE THE CARDS TO RANDOMIZE THE REST. MAKE ADJUSTMENTS IF TOO MANY SIMILAR LOOKING ITEMS OCCUR TOGETHER. FOR KNOWLEDGE BASED QUESTIONNAIRES WHICH HAVE ITEMS OF INCREASING DIFFICULTY ORDER THE ITEMS FROM EASY TO HARD.

Designing the questionnaire

Good design is crucial for producing a reliable and valid questionnaire. Respondents feel less intimidated by a questionnaire which has a clear layout and is easy to understand, and take their task of completing the questionnaire more seriously.

BACKGROUND INFORMATION. Include headings and sufficient space for the respondent to fill in his or her name, age, sex or whatever other background information you require. It is often useful to obtain the date on which the questionnaire is completed, especially if it is to be administered again.

INSTRUCTIONS. The instructions must be clear and unambiguous. They should tell the respondent how to choose a response and how to indicate the chosen response on the questionnaire. Other relevant instructions should be given, e.g. respond as quickly as possible, respond to every item or respond as honestly as possible. Information which is likely to increase compliance, e.g. regarding confidentiality, should be stressed.

Sample instructions for a knowledge based multiple choice questionnaire:

INSTRUCTIONS: Each item is followed by a choice of possible responses: A, B, C, D or E. Read each item carefully and decide which choice *best* answers the question. Indicate your answer by circling the letter responding to your choice. Your score will be the number of correct answers so respond to each question even if you are not sure of the correct answer.

Sample instructions for a person based rating scale questionnaire:

INSTRUCTIONS: Each statement is followed by a series of possible responses: strongly disagree, disagree, agree or strongly agree. Read each statement carefully and decide which response best describes how you feel. Then put a tick over the corresponding response. Please respond to every statement. If you are not completely sure which response is more accurate, put the response which you feel is most appropriate. Do not spend too long on each statement. It is important that you answer each question as honestly as possible. *ALL INFORMATION WILL BE TREATED WITH THE STRICTEST CONFIDENCE.*

LAYOUT. The following tips will help you to arrange items on the page so that they are easy to read:

155

(a) Number each item.

(b) Keep each line short with no more than 10 or 12 words on a line.

(c) Ensure that the items produce a straight vertical margin down the left-hand side of the page.

1. — — — — — — — — — — — — — — — — — —
2. — — — — — — — — — — — — — — —
3. —
   — — — — — — —
4. — — — — — — — — — — — — — —
5. — — — — — — — — — — — — — — — —

(d) Arrange the response options to produce a straight vertical margin down the right-hand side of the page. Insert headings at the top and symbols next to each item. There should be a clear visual relationship between each item and its response options. This can be done by inserting a dotted line from the item stem to its response option.

	STRONGLY DISAGREE	DISAGREE	AGREE	STRONGLY AGREE
1. — — — — — — — — — — — —	SD	D	A	SA
2. — — — — — — —	SD	D	A	SA
3. — — — — — — — — — — — — — —				
— — — — — — —	SD	D	A	SA
4. — — — — — — — — —	SD	D	A	SA

(e) Separate each item with a space rather than a horizontal line. If your items, instructions and background information all fit on one page, then good. However, it is better to produce a neat 2 or 3 page questionnaire than one page which looks cramped.

(f) If using more than one type of item, group similar items together. Each type will need different instructions and response options.

(g) Have the questionnaire printed or typed with a smart typewriter. Ensure that the type is large enough to be read easily. Capitals are difficult to read and should not be used for the item stems. However, capitals can be used for headings to make them stand out. Word processors are excellent for planning a layout as you can experiment with different sizes of type and different spacings to see which look best.

(h) You can use design as a tool to portray or disguise the purpose of your questionnaire. For example, small closely set type can make a questionnaire look very formal while larger type with items spaced well apart on coloured paper is friendlier. Design can set an atmosphere — use it!

THE GRIMS was designed with simplicity of administration in mind. The respondent has to answer 28 questions on one side of paper with the same response options for each question. This makes it quick and uncomplicated to complete.

TRY WRITING OUT YOUR QUESTIONNAIRE ON PAPER OR TYPING IT OUT ON A WORD PROCESSOR SCREEN UNTIL THE ARRANGEMENT LOOKS LOGICAL. THEN EXPERIMENT WITH SIZE OF TYPE, SPACING AND NUMBER OF PAGES TO SEE WHAT LOOKS BEST.

To score your questionnaire, allocate a score to each response option and then add up the score for each item to give a total score for the questionnaire.

For knowledge based questionnaires, it is usual to give the correct or best option for each item a score of 1 and the distractor options a score of 0. The higher the total score, the better the performance.

For person based questionnaires, scores should be allocated to response options according to a continuous scale, e.g. always = 5, usually = 4, occasionally = 3, hardly ever = 2, never = 1; yes = 2, uncertain = 1, no = 0; true = 1, false = 0. For reversed items, it is necessary to reverse the scoring (e.g. always = 1, usually = 2, occasionally = 3, hardly ever = 4, never = 5) so that each item is scored in the same direction. After reversing the scores, add up the score for each item to obtain the total score for the questionnaire. Depending on the way in which you have allocated scores to response options, the higher the total score, the greater or lesser the presence of the characteristic being measured.

A scoring key which fits over the questionnaire to identify which option the respondent has chosen for each item and its score can be useful for quick and easy scoring. In the example below, the respondent has obtained a total score of 10 (3 + 3 + 1 + 3).

STRONGLY DISAGREE   DISAGREE   AGREE   STRONGLY AGREE

1. — — — — — — — — — — — .... ○ ○ ● ○
     1   2   3   4

2. — — — — — — — .... ○ ● ○ ○
     4   3   2   1

3. — — — — — — — — — .... ○ ○ ○ ●
     4   3   2   1

4. — — — — — — .... ○ ○ ● ○
     1   2   3   4

Simple computer programs can also be written for scoring questionnaires. This method is particularly useful for scoring large numbers of questionnaires.

Piloting the questionnaire

The next stage in constructing your questionnaire is the pilot study. This involves having the questionnaire completed by people who are similar to those for whom the questionnaire is intended. Analysis of these data will help you to select the best items for the final version of your questionnaire.

If, for example, your questionnaire is intended for married women with pre-school children you might carry out the pilot study at a baby clinic or a mothers and toddlers club. If it is for use with the general population, you would need to find a group of people who are representative of the population at large. This is often more difficult than finding a more specific group. You could make use of the electoral register, which is available from libraries, but this is usually too time consuming to be worth while for a pilot study. When a truly representative group is impossible to find, an approximation is usually good enough. A common strategy is to hand out questionnaires in public places such as shopping centres, train and bus stations, airport lounges, doctors' waiting rooms, or canteens of large organizations. The respondents who take part in the pilot study should vary in terms of demographic characteristics such as age, sex and social class. There is little point in piloting a questionnaire intended for both sexes only with men, or a questionnaire to be used with all social classes only with manual workers and not managers. It is important to obtain relevant demographic information from the respondents in the pilot study to help with the validation of your questionnaire at a later stage.

The pilot version of your questionnaire should be administered to as many people as possible. The minimum number of respondents required is one more than the number of items. If it is not possible to obtain this many, it is better to use fewer people than to omit the piloting stage altogether.

The pilot version of the GRIMS was administered to both partners in 60 client couples from marital therapy and marriage guidance clinics throughout the country

ADMINISTER YOUR QUESTIONNAIRE AND OBTAIN RELEVANT DEMOGRAPHIC INFORMATION FROM A GROUP OF PEOPLE WHO ARE SIMILAR TO THOSE FOR WHOM THE FINAL QUESTIONNAIRE IS INTENDED.

Item analysis

Item analysis of the data collected in the pilot study to select the best items for the final version of your questionnaire involves an examination of the FACILITY and the DISCRIMINATION of each item. For knowledge based multiple choice items it is also important to look at DISTRACTORS.

The first step is to draw an item analysis table with each column (a, b, c, d, e, etc.) representing an item and each row (1, 2, 3, 4, 5, etc.) representing a respondent. For knowledge based items, insert '1' in each cell for which the respondent gave the correct answer, and '0' for an incorrect answer. For person based items, insert the actual score for each item remembering to ensure that reversed items are scored in the same direction as non-reversed items. Add up the score for each cell to give a total score for each row (i.e. each subject) and a total score for each column (i.e. each item).

Sample item analysis table for knowledge based questionnaire:

		Items					
		a	b	c	d	e	Sum
	1	1	1	0	1	1	4
	2	0	1	0	0	1	2
Respondents	3	1	0	0	1	1	3
	4	1	0	0	0	1	2
	5	0	0	0	1	1	2
	Sum	3	2	0	3	5	13

FACILITY: Most questionnaires are designed to differentiate respondents according to whatever knowledge or characteristic is being measured (see discussion of norm and criterion reference testing in Chapter 3). A good item, therefore, is one for which different respondents give different responses. The facility index gives an indication of the extent to which respondents answer an item in the same way. These items are redundant and it is important to get rid of them. For example, if every respondent gives the correct response to a particular item, this simply has the effect of adding one point to the total score for each respondent and does not discriminate among them.

For knowledge based questionnaires, the facility index is calculated by dividing the number of respondents who obtain the correct response for an item by the total number of respondents. Ideally, the facility index for each item should lie between 0.25 and 0.75, averaging 0.5 for the entire questionnaire. A facility index of less than 0.25 indicates that the item is too difficult as very few respondents obtain the correct response; and a facility index of more than 0.75 shows that the item is too easy as most respondents obtain the correct response. For the sample item analysis table above, the facility index for each item is as follows: (a) $3/5 = 0.6$ (b) $2/5 = 0.4$ (c) $0/5 = 0$ (d) $3/5 = 0.6$ and (e) $5/5 = 1$. Here we would probably wish to eliminate items (c) and (e) from the final questionnaire as everyone has responded to these items in the same way.

Similarly, the facility index for person based items is calculated by summing the score for the item for each respondent, and then dividing this total by the total number of respondents. An item with a facility index which is equal to or approaching either of the extreme scores for the item should not be included in the final version of the questionnaire. It is also important to ensure by looking at the scores in the item analysis table that a good facility index, i.e. lying somewhere between the extreme scores, does not simply mean that everyone has chosen the middle option.

DISCRIMINATION: This is the ability of each item to discriminate respondents according to whatever the questionnaire is measuring, i.e. respondents who perform well on a knowledge based questionnaire or who exhibit the characteristic being measured by a person based questionnaire should respond to each item in a particular way. Items should only be selected for the final version of the questionnaire if they measure the same knowledge or characteristic as the other items in the questionnaire.

Discrimination is measured by correlating each item with the total score for the questionnaire. The higher the correlation coefficient, the more discriminating the item. There are no hard and fast rules about inclusion criteria for items in the final questionnaire. It is usual to choose 70–80% of the original items. The higher the correlation between the item and the overall questionnaire the better, and a minimum correlation of 0.2 is generally required. Items with negative or zero correlations are almost always excluded.

The Pearson product–moment formula is generally used to calculate the correlation coefficient between each item and the total score for the questionnaire. The score for each respondent for an item is correlated with the total score for each respondent for the questionnaire. This can be calculated easily by computer. If a computer is not available the formula below can be used to calculate the Pearson product–moment correlation coefficient by hand. Remember that correlation coefficients always lie between 1 and -1. If you obtain a coefficient outwith this range then you have made a mistake in your calculation.

Pearson product–moment formula

$$r = \frac{n \, \Sigma XY - (\Sigma X)(\Sigma Y)}{\sqrt{[n \, \Sigma X^2 - (\Sigma X)^2][n \, \Sigma Y^2 - (\Sigma Y)^2]}},$$

r = the product–moment correlation coefficient
X = each of the scores on the item
Y = each of the scores on the questionnaire
n = the number of pairs of scores
Σ = the sum

In order to compute the Pearson product–moment correlation coefficient, you will need the sum of the respondents' scores on the item (ΣX), the sum of the respondents' scores on the total questionnaire (ΣY), the sum of the squares of the respondents' scores on the item (ΣX^2), the sum of the squares of the respondents' scores on the total questionnaire (ΣY^2), and the sum of the products of the scores on the item and the total questionnaire (ΣXY). Putting these figures into the formula will enable you to calculate the correlation coefficient. The following example shows an easy way of doing this. Remember to repeat the calculation for each item.

Respon-dents	Score on item	Score on item squared	Score on qu'aire	Score on qu'aire squared	Score on item × score on qu'aire
n	(X)	(X^2)	(Y)	(Y^2)	(XY)
1	1	1	30	900	30
2	3	9	57	3,249	171
3	5	25	94	8,836	470
4	4	16	76	5,776	304
5	3	9	80	6,400	240
6	1	1	33	1,089	33
7	2	4	54	2,916	108
8	2	4	58	3,364	116
9	5	25	83	6,889	415
10	4	6	76	5,776	304
	$\Sigma X = 30$	$\Sigma X^2 = 110$	$\Sigma Y = 641$	$\Sigma Y^2 = 45,195$	$\Sigma XY = 2,191$

$$r = \frac{10\,(2{,}191) - (30)\,(641)}{\sqrt{[\,10\,(110) - (30)^2\,]\,[\,10\,(45{,}195) - (641)^2\,]}}$$

$$= \frac{21{,}910 - 19{,}230}{\sqrt{[\,1{,}100 - 900\,]\,[\,451{,}950 - 410{,}881\,]}}$$

$$= \frac{2{,}680}{\sqrt{(200)\,(41{,}069)}}$$

$$= \frac{2{,}680}{\sqrt{8{,}213{,}800}}$$

$$= \frac{2{,}680}{2{,}866}$$

$$= 0.935$$

DISTRACTORS: An examination of the use of distractor options by respondents who do not choose the correct or best option should be carried out for each item to ensure that each distractor is endorsed by a similar proportion of respondents. This can be done by inserting the endorsed option for incorrect items into the item analysis table for each respondent and simply looking at the pattern of responses for each item. Items for which distractor options are not functioning should be considered for exclusion from the final questionnaire.

When deciding which items to include in the final version of your questionnaire you will have to take many factors into account and balance one against another. In addition to facility, discrimination and distractors, you will need to consider the number of items you require for the final version (at least 20 are necessary for a reliable questionnaire), and how well the items fit the blueprint. For example, you might include an item with fairly poor discrimination if you have very few items from that area of the blueprint, or you might include an item with poor facility if it has reasonable discrimination. It is also important to ensure that there are approximately equal numbers of reversed and non-reversed items. Ways of improving items may become clear at this stage. For example, changing the wording of an item from 'sometimes' to 'always' may improve facility. However, it is not a good idea to change very many items as you will not know how these changes affect the reliability and validity of the questionnaire. The procedures of item analysis will inform you about the characteristics of each item. It is then up to you to decide which criteria are most important for the purpose of your particular questionnaire.

DECIDE WHICH ITEMS FROM THE PILOT VERSION OF YOUR QUESTIONNAIRE TO INCLUDE IN THE FINAL VERSION TAKING ACCOUNT OF FACILITY, DISCRIMINATION AND, IF APPROPRIATE, DISTRACTORS. ORDER THE ITEMS AND DESIGN THE QUESTIONNAIRE AS BEFORE.

Reliability

Reliability is an estimate of the accuracy of a questionnaire. For example, a questionnaire is reliable if a respondent obtains a similar score on different occasions, providing the respondent has not changed in a way which affects his or her response to the questionnaire. There are several ways of measuring reliability: TEST–RETEST, PARALLEL FORMS and SPLIT HALF.

TEST–RETEST. This involves administering the same questionnaire to the same respondents under the same circumstances on two occasions and correlating the scores. A problem with this method is that respondents may remember their responses on the second occasion, so it is a good idea to separate the two administrations of the questionnaire as much as possible.

PARALLEL FORMS. In this case it is necessary to construct two equivalent forms of the questionnaire and to administer both to the same respondents in order to correlate the scores. The main difficulty is in selecting two equivalent sets of items.

SPLIT HALF. Here the questionnaire is divided into two halves (usually odd items and even items) and the correlation between the halves is used to produce an estimate of reliability for the whole questionnaire. This method does not give reliability over a period of time.

For test–retest reliability and parallel forms, the correlation coefficient is calculated with the Pearson product–moment formula. This procedure is described in the section on item analysis. For split half reliability, the Pearson product–moment coefficient between the two halves of the questionnaire is used in the Spearman–Brown formula to give an estimate of reliability for the whole questionnaire.

Spearman–Brown formula

$$r_{11} = \frac{2r_{\frac{1}{2}\frac{1}{2}}}{1 + r_{\frac{1}{2}\frac{1}{2}}}$$

r_{11} = estimated reliability for the whole questionnaire
$r_{\frac{1}{2}\frac{1}{2}}$ = correlation between two halves of the questionnaire

For example, if the Pearson product–moment correlation coefficient between two halves of a questionnaire is 0.80:

$$r_{11} = \frac{2(0.80)}{1 + 0.80} = 0.88.$$

It has been argued that the best procedure for obtaining a measure of reliability is to administer parallel forms several weeks or months apart. However, this can be extremely time consuming and split half reliability is more commonly used. This provides an estimate of reliability from one administration of the same test, and can be carried out with data collected in the pilot study. The greater the number of respondents, the better the estimate of reliability. If less than 50 respondents were included in the pilot study, it is necessary to have the final version of the questionnaire completed by more people, ensuring once again that they are similar to those for whom the questionnaire is intended. Ideally, data from at least 200 respondents should be used in calculating reliability. Where the questionnaire is intended for different types of respondents, it is usual to show that it is reliable for each type. In this case, a total of 200 respondents would be needed altogether. Whatever measure of reliability is used, a coefficient of at least 0.7 is generally required for person based questionnaires and at least 0.8 for knowledge based questionnaires.

> *For the GRIMS, split half reliabilities were obtained for men and women separately for the respondents in the pilot study, marital therapy clients and a general population group. Reliabilities ranged from 0.81 to 0.94. Test–retest reliability was also calculated for marital therapy clients before and after therapy. Not surprisingly, these were much lower as the clients showed considerable change as a result of therapy.*

CALCULATE THE SPLIT HALF RELIABILITY FOR THE FINAL VERSION OF YOUR QUESTIONNAIRE USING DATA FROM THE RELEVANT ITEMS FROM ALL OF THE RESPONDENTS IN THE PILOT STUDY PLUS ADDITIONAL RESPONDENTS IF NECESSARY. FOR EACH RESPONDENT, CALCULATE THE TOTAL SCORE FOR THE EVEN ITEMS IN THE FINAL VERSION OF YOUR QUESTIONNAIRE AND THE TOTAL SCORE FOR THE ODD ITEMS. CORRELATE THE ODD ITEMS WITH THE EVEN ITEMS USING THE PEARSON PRODUCT–MOMENT FORMULA. USE THIS CORRELATION COEFFICIENT IN THE SPEARMAN–BROWN FORMULA TO OBTAIN AN ESTIMATE OF RELIABILITY FOR THE WHOLE QUESTIONNAIRE.

Validity

The validity of a questionnaire is the extent to which it measures what it is intended to measure. Validity must be determined, therefore, in relation to the purpose of the questionnaire. There are several types of validity of which the most straightforward are: FACE VALIDITY, CONTENT VALIDITY, CRITERION RELATED VALIDITY and PREDICTIVE VALIDITY.

FACE VALIDITY. This describes the appearance of the questionnaire to respondents, i.e. whether or not it looks as if it is measuring what it claims to measure. If not, respondents may not take the questionnaire seriously.

CONTENT VALIDITY. This is the relationship between the content and the purpose of the questionnaire, i.e. whether or not there is a good match between the test specification and the task specification. For example, the blueprint for a questionnaire used in job selection should match the job description.

CRITERION RELATED VALIDITY. This is the relationship between scores on the questionnaire and a criterion measure. For example, with a marital problems questionnaire we would expect couples on the verge of separation to obtain a score which is indicative of marital distress. It is important to select a criterion measure which is relevant, reliable and available.

PREDICTIVE VALIDITY. This is similar to criterion related validity but relates scores on a questionnaire to a future criterion measure. For example, the predictive validity of a job selection questionnaire can be calculated by correlating questionnaire scores with future achievement at work, and the predictive validity of a marital problems questionnaire can be calculated by correlating questionnaire scores with future separation or divorce.

For your questionnaire to have face validity, you must ensure that it looks reasonable to the respondents for whom it is intended. Content validity is generally taken care of in constructing the blueprint and in the item analysis. However, it is important to check that the balance of items in the final version of your questionnaire matches the original blueprint. Criterion related validity and predictive validity are obtained by correlating the questionnaire score with a criterion measure for a group of at least 50 respondents. The higher the correlation coefficient, the better the validity. The Pearson product–moment correlation formula is generally used to calculate the correlation coefficient.

Content validity of the GRIMS is high with respect to its specification, and good face validity has been incorporated into the item selection. It is also important for the GRIMS to have good diagnostic validity. This was established by determining that couples who presented at marriage guidance clinics had significantly higher scores than a matched sample from the general population. Moreover, couples presenting for marital therapy had significantly higher scores than couples presenting for sex therapy. Because the GRIMS was intended as a measure of improvement after therapy, it was important to

167

obtain a rating of the validity of the GRIMS as an estimator of change. Couples were asked to complete the GRIMS before and after therapy, and the therapists, who were blind to their clients' GRIMS scores, were asked to rate the couple on a 5 point scale ranging from '0 – improved a great deal' to '4 – got worse'. The GRIMS scores for the male and female partner were averaged for each couple. The average score before therapy was subtracted from the average score following therapy to give a change score representing change during therapy. The change scores were correlated with the therapists' ratings of change giving a correlation coefficient of 0.77. This is firm evidence for the validity of change in the GRIMS score as an estimate of change in the quality of the relationship, or in the effectiveness of therapy.

ENSURE THAT YOUR QUESTIONNAIRE HAS GOOD FACE VALIDITY, CONTENT VALIDITY, CRITERION RELATED VALIDITY AND/OR PREDICTIVE VALIDITY AS WELL AS ANY OTHER RELEVANT TYPES OF VALIDITY SUCH AS DIAGNOSTIC VALIDITY OR VALIDITY OF CHANGE SCORES.

Standardization

Standardization involves obtaining scores on the final version of your questionnaire from appropriate groups of respondents. These scores are called norms. Large numbers of respondents must be carefully selected according to clearly specified criteria in order for norms to be meaningful.

With good norms it is possible to interpret the score of an individual respondent, i.e. whether or not his or her score on the questionnaire is typical. This is useful if, for example, you wish to know how an individual child performs on an ability test compared with other children of the same age, or if you wish to determine how a person with a suspected clinical disorder compares with patients who have been diagnosed as having that disorder.

It is not always necessary to produce norms. If your questionnaire has been developed for research which involves comparing groups of respondents, norms can be useful in interpreting the performance of a group as a whole, but they are not crucial. If, however, you wish to interpret the score of an individual, it is necessary to have good norms against which to compare an individual score.

It is important to include as many respondents as possible in the standardization group, and to ensure that the respondents are truly representative. A minimum of several hundred is generally required but this depends to a large extent on the nature of the respondents. Some are easier to find than others, and it is often better to obtain a smaller group of very appropriate respondents than a larger but less appropriate one. In some cases it is necessary to obtain several standardization groups, or to stratify the standardization group according to relevant variables such as age, sex or social class. Ideally, there should be several hundred respondents in each group or stratification. Norms should be presented in terms of the mean and standard deviation for each group or stratification.

Mean

$$\bar{X} = \frac{X}{n}$$

$\bar{X}$ = mean score
X = each of the scores on the total questionnaire
n = number of respondents
    = sum

Standard deviation

$$SD = \sqrt{\frac{n\ X^2 - (\ X)^2}{n\,(n - 1)}}$$

SD = standard deviation
X = each of the scores on the total questionnaire
n = number of respondents
     = sum

The following example shows an easy way of doing this.

X	X^2
3	9
4	16
7	49
8	64
8	64
9	81
10	100
$\Sigma X = 49$	$\Sigma X^2 = 383$
$n = 7$	

$$\text{mean} = \frac{49}{7}$$

$$= 7$$

$$\text{standard deviation} = \sqrt{\frac{7\,(383) - (49)^2}{7\,(7 - 1)}}$$

$$= \sqrt{\frac{2681 - 2401}{42}}$$

$$= \sqrt{\frac{280}{42}}$$

$$= \sqrt{6.67}$$

$$= 2.58$$

The GRIMS was standardized using two groups (i) a random sample of people attending their family doctor with the usual variety of medical problems (a general population group), and (ii) clients attending marriage guidance clinics and marital and sexual therapy clinics (a marital problems group).

STANDARDIZE YOUR QUESTIONNAIRE USING A RELEVANT GROUP OR GROUPS OF AS MANY RESPONDENTS AS POSSIBLE. PRESENT THE NORMS IN TERMS OF THE MEAN AND STANDARD DEVIATION FOR EACH GROUP OR STRATIFICATION.

Bibliography

Anastasi, A. (1982), *Psychological Testing*, 5th edn, New York: Macmillan.

Angoff, W.H. and Ford, S.F. (1973), *Journal of Educational Measurement*, 10, 95–106.

Atkinson, R.C. and Wilson, H.A. (1969), *Computer Assisted Instruction: A Book of Readings*, New York: Academic Press.

Barclay, J.R. (1983), *Barclay Classroom Assessment System Manual*, Los Angeles: Western Psychological Services.

Beck, A.T., Ward, C.H., Mendelson, M., Mock, J., and Erbaugh, J. (1961), 'An inventory for measuring depression', *Archives of General Psychiatry*, 4, 53–63.

Bennun, I., Rust, J., and Golombok, S. (1985), 'The effects of marital therapy on sexual satisfaction', *Scandinavian Journal of Behaviour Therapy*, 14(2), 65–72.

Berk, R.A. (1984), *A Guide to Criterion-Referenced Test Construction*, Baltimore, Maryland: Johns Hopkins University Press.

Berk, R.A. (1986), 'Minimum competency testing: Status and potential', in B.S. Plake and J.C. Witt (eds), *The Future of Testing*, Hillsdale, New Jersey: Erlbaum, 89–144.

Birnbaum, A. (1968), 'Some latent trait models and their use in inferring an examinee's ability', in F.M. Lord and M.R. Novick (eds), *Statistical Theories of Mental Test Scores*, Reading, Massachusetts: Addison-Wesley.

Bloom, B. (1956), *Taxonomy of Educational Objectives, Handbook I: Cognitive Domain*, New York: Longmans, Green & Co.

Bock, R.D. and Mislevy, R.J. (1982), 'Adaptive EAP estimation of ability in a microcomputer environment', *Applied Psychological Measurement*, 6, 431–44.

Broadfoot, P. (1986), *Profiles and Records of Achievement*, Eastbourne, England: Holt, Rinehart & Winston.

Buros, O.K., *The Mental Measurement Yearbooks*, vols I–VIII, Gryphon Press.

Carnap, R. (1962), *Logical Foundations of Probability*, 2nd edn, Chicago: University of Chicago Press.

Cattell, R.B. (1965), *The Scientific Analysis of Personality*, London, England: Penguin.

Chambers, W. and Chambers, R. (1972), *Chambers Twentieth Century Dictionary*, Edinburgh, Scotland: Chambers.

Cleary, T.A. (1968), 'Test bias: Prediction of grades of Negro and white students in integrated colleges', *Journal of Educational Measurement*, 5, 115–24.

Cleary, T.A. and Hilton, T.G. (1968), 'An investigation of item bias', *Educational and Psychological Measurement*, 28, 61–75.

Cole, N. (1973), 'Bias in selection', *Journal of Educational Measurement*, 10, 237–55.

Cronbach, L.J., Gleser, G.C., Nanda, H., and Rajaratnan, N. (1972), *The Dependability of Behavioral Measurements: Theory of Generalizability for Scores and Profiles*, New York: Wiley.

Darlington, C. (1971), 'Another look at "cultural fairness" ', *Journal of Educational and Psychological Measurement*, 8, 71–82.

Darwin, C. (1888), *The Descent of Man*, 2nd edn, London, England: John Murray.

Debra P. v Turlington, 644 F.2.d 397, 404 (5th Cir 1981).

Einhorn, H. and Bass, A. (1971), 'Methodological considerations relevant to discrimination in employment testing', *Psychological Bulletin*, 75, 261–9.

Elliot, C.D. (1983), *British Ability Scales Technical Handbook*, Windsor, England: NFER-Nelson.

Eysenck, H.J. (1967), *The Biological Basis of Personality*, Springfield, Illinois: Thomas Books.

Eysenck, H.J. (1973), *The Inequality of Man*, London, England: Maurice Temple-Smith.

Eysenck, H.J. (1986), 'The theory of intelligence and the psychophysiology of cognition', in R.J. Sternberg (ed.), *Advances in the Psychology of Human Intelligence*, vol. 3, Hillsdale, New Jersey: Erlbaum, 1–34.

Eysenck, S.B.G., Rust, J., and Eysenck, H.J. (1977), 'Personality and the classification of adult offenders', *British Journal of Criminology*, 17(2), 169–79.

Ferguson, G.A. (1981), *Statistical Analysis in Psychology and Education*, 4th edn, New York: McGraw-Hill.

Galton, F. (1869), *Hereditary Genius*, London, England: Macmillan.

Gipps, C. (1986), 'A critique of the APU', in D.L. Nuttall (ed.), *Assessing Educational Achievement*, Lewes, England: Falmer Press.

Golden, C.J., Hammeke, T.A., and Purisch, A.D. (1978), 'Diagnostic validity of a standardized neuropsychological battery derived from Luria's neuropsychological tests', *Journal of Consulting and Clinical Psychology*, 46, 1258–65.

Golden, C.J. (1981), 'A standardised version of Luria's neuropsychological tests: A quantitative and qualitative approach to neuropsychological evaluation', in S.B. Filskov and T.J. Bolls (eds), *Handbook of Clinical Neuropsychology*, New York: Wiley.

173

Golombok, S., Rust, J., and Pickard, C. (1984), 'Sexual problems encountered in general practice', *British Journal of Sexual Medicine*, 11, 171–5.

Greg, W.R. (1868), *Fraser's Magazine*, September 1868.

Griggs v. Duke Power Co., 401 US. 424 (1971).

Gross, A.L. and Su, W. (1975), 'Defining a "fair" or "unbiased" selection model: a question of utilities', *Journal of Applied Psychology* 60, 345–51.

Guilford, J.P. (1959), *Personality*, New York: McGraw-Hill.

Haladyna, T.M. and Roid, G.H. (1983), 'A comparison of two approaches to criterion referenced test construction', *Journal of Educational Measurement*, 20, 271–82.

Hambleton, R.K. and Swaminathan, H. (1985), *Item Response Theory: Principles and Applications*, Boston: Kluwer-Nijhoff.

Hathaway, S.R. and McKinley, J.C. (1965), *Minnesota Multiphasic Personality Inventory: Manual for Administration and Scoring*, New York: The Psychological Corporation.

Hendrickson, A.E. (1982a), 'The biological basis of intelligence. Part 1: Theory', in H.J. Eysenck (ed.), *A Model for Intelligence*, New York: Springer Verlag.

Hendrickson, A.E. (1982b), 'The biological basis of intelligence. Part 2: Measurement', in H.J. Eysenck (ed.), *A Model for Intelligence*, New York: Springer Verlag.

Jensen, A.R. (1973), *Educability and Group Differences*, London, England: Methuen.

Jensen, A.R. (1980), *Bias in Mental Testing*, New York: Macmillan.

Kamin, L.J. (1974), *The Science and Politics of IQ*, New York: Wiley.

Kitcher, P. (1985), *Vaulting Ambition: Sociobiology and the Quest for Human Nature*, Cambridge, Massachusetts: MIT Press.

Klinger, D.E., Johnson, J.H., and Williams, T.A. (1976), 'Strategies in the evaluation of an on-line computer-assisted unit for intake assessment of mental health patients', *Behavior Research Methods and Instrumentation*, 8, 95–100.

Lachar, D. (1974), 'Accuracy and generalizability of an automated MMPI interpretation system', *Journal of Consulting and Clinical Psychology*, 42, 267–73.

Loevinger, J. (1957), 'Objective tests as instruments of psychological theory', *Psychological Reports*, 3, 635–94.

Lord, F.M. (1977), 'A study of item bias using item characteristic curve theory', in Y.H. Poortinga (ed.), *Basic Problems in Cross-Cultural Psychology*, Amsterdam: Swets & Zeitlinger.

Lord, F.M. and Novick, M.R. (1968), *Statistical Theories of Mental Test Scores*, Reading, Massachusetts: Addison-Wesley.

Luria, A.R. (1973), *The Working Brain*, London, England: Penguin.

McClelland, J.L. and Rumelhart, D.E. (1987), *Parallel Distributed Processing: Explorations in the Microstructure of Cognition. Volume 2: Psychological and Biological Models*, London, England: MIT Press.

McDermott, P.A. (1980), 'A systems-actuarial method for differential diagnosis of handicapped children', *Journal of Special Education*, 50, 223–8.

Nie, N.H. *et al.* (1983), *SPSSX User Guide*, Chicago: SPSS Inc.

Peterson, N. (1980), 'Bias in the selection rule — bias in the test', in L.J.T. van der Kamp, W.F. Langerak, and D.N.M. de Gruijter (eds), *Psychometrics for Educational Debates*, Chichester, England: Wiley, 103–22.

Popham, W.J. (1978), *Criterion-referenced Measurement*, Englewood Cliffs, New Jersey: Prentice-Hall.

Popper, K.R. (1972), *The Logic of Scientific Discovery*, Tiptree, Essex, England: Anchor Press.

Rasch, G. (1980), *Probabilistic Models for Intelligence and Attainment Testing*, Chicago: University of Chicago Press.

Reitan, R.M. (1955), 'An investigation of the validity of Halstead's measures of biological intelligence', *Archives of Neurology and Psychiatry*, 73, 28–35.

Roid, G.H. (1986), 'Computer technology in testing', in B.S. Plake and J.C. Witt (eds), *The Future of Testing*, Hillsdale, New Jersey: Erlbaum, 29–69.

Rorschach, H. (1942), *Psychodiagnostics: A Diagnostic Test Based on Perception*, transl. by P. Lemkau and B. Kroenburg, Berne: Huber (1st German edn, 1921; USA distributor, Grune & Stratton).

Rumelhart, D.E. and McClelland, J.L. (1986), *Parallel Distributed Processing: Explorations in the Microstructure of Cognition. Volume 1: Foundations*, London, England: MIT Press.

Rust, J. (1974), 'Interactions of reliabilities in personality measurement', *Social Behaviour and Personality*, 2(1), 108–10.

Rust, J. (1975a), 'Genetic effects in the auditory cortical evoked potential: A twin study', *Electroencephalography and Clinical Neurophysiology*, 39(4), 321–7.

Rust, J. (1975b) 'Cortical evoked potential, personality and intelligence', *Journal of Comparative and Physiological Psychology*, 89(10), 1220–6.

Rust, J. (1984), 'Genetic sources of variation in electrodermal measures: A twin study,' *Indian Journal of Psychophysiology*, 2, 12–20.

Rust, J. (1987), 'The Rust Inventory of Schizoid Cognitions (RISC): A psychometric measure of psychoticism in the general population', *British Journal of Clinical Psychology*, 26(2), 151–2.

Rust, J. (1988a), *Handbook of the Rust Inventory of Schizotypal Cognitions*, London, England: The Psychological Corporation.

Rust, J. (1988b), 'The Rust Inventory of Schizotypal Cognitions', *Schizophrenia Bulletin* (in press).

Rust, J., Bennun, I., Crowe, M., and Golombok, S. (1988), *Handbook of the Golombok Rust Inventory of Marital State (GRIMS)*, Windsor, England: NFER Nelson.

Rust, J. and Golombok, S. (1985), 'The Golombok Rust Inventory of Sexual Satisfaction (GRISS)', *British Journal of Clinical Psychology*, 24(1), 63–4.

Rust, J. and Golombok, S. (1986a), 'The GRISS: A psychometric instrument for the assessment of sexual dysfunction', *Archives of Sexual Behaviour*, 15(2), 153–61.

Rust, J. and Golombok, S. (1986b), *The Golombok Rust Inventory of Sexual Satisfaction (GRISS)*, Windsor, England: NFER Nelson.

Scheuneman, J. (1975), 'A new method of assessing bias in test items', paper presented at the meeting of the American Educational Research Association, Washington, April 1975, ERIC Document Reproduction Service No. ED 106-359.

Scheuneman, J. (1980), 'Latent-trait theory and item bias', in L.J.T. van der Kamp, W.F. Langerak and D.N.M. de Gruijter (eds), *Psychometrics for Educational Debates*, Chichester, England: Wiley, 139–51.

Spearman, C. (1904), 'General intelligence: objectively determined and measured', *American Journal of Psychology*, 115, 201–92.

Spearman, C. and Wynn-Jones, L. (1950), *Human Ability*, London, England: Macmillan.

Sternberg, R.J. (1977), *Intelligence, Information Processing, and Analogical Reasoning: The Componential Analysis of Human Abilities*, Hillsdale New Jersey: Erlbaum.

Sutcliffe, J.P. (1965), 'A probability model for errors of classification. I: General considerations', *Psychometrika*, 30, 73–96.

Terman, L.M. (1919), *Measurement of Intelligence*, London, England: Harrap.

Thorndike, R.L. (1947), *Research Problems and Techniques*, Report No. 3 AAF Aviation Psychology Program Research Reports, Washington: US Government Printing Office.

Thorndike, R.L. (1964) 'Reliability', in *Proceedings of the 1963 Invitational Conference on Testing Problems*, Princetown, New Jersey: Educational Testing Service, 23–32.

Thorndike, R.L. (1971), 'Concepts of culture-fairness', *Journal of Educational Measurement*, 8, 63–70.

Thorndike, R.L. and Hagen, E.P. (1977), *Measurement and Evaluation in Psychology and Education*, 4th edn, New York: Wiley.

Thurstone, L.L. (1947), *Multiple Factor Analysis: A Development and Expansion of Vectors of the Mind*, Chicago: Chicago University Press.

Tversky, A. and Kahneman, D. (1983), 'Extensional versus intuitive reasoning: The conjunction fallacy in probability judgement', *Psychological Review*, 90, 293–315.

van der Kamp, L.J., Langerak, W.F., and de Gruijter, D.N.M. (eds) (1980), *Psychometrics for Educational Debates*, Chichester, England: Wiley.

Wason, P.C. and Johnson-Laird, P.N. (1972), *The Psychology of Reasoning: Structure in Content*, Cambridge, Massachusetts: Harvard University Press.

Wechsler, D.W. (1958), *The Measurement and Appraisal of Adult Intelligence*, 4th edn, Baltimore: Williams & Wilkins.

Wilson, E.O. (1975), *Sociobiology: The New Synthesis*, Cambridge,

Massachusetts: Harvard University Press.

Wilson, G.D., Rust, J., and Kasriel, J. (1977), 'Genetic and family origins of humour preferences: A twin study', *Psychological Reports*, 41(2), 659–60.

Winer, B.J. (1962), *Statistical Principles in Experimental Design*, New York: McGraw-Hill.

Wittgenstein, L. (1958), *Philosophical Investigations*, London, England: Blackwell.

Wright, B.D. and Masters, G.N. (1982), *Rating Scale Analysis: Rasch Measurement*, Chicago: MESA Press.

Zachary, R.A. and Gorsuch, R.L. (1985), 'Continuous norming: Implications for the WAIS-R', *Journal of Clinical Psychology*, 41, 86–94.

Zachary, R.A. and Pope, K.S. (1983), 'Legal and ethical issues in the clinical use of computerized testing', in M.D. Schartz (ed.), *Using Computers in Clinical Practice*, New York: Haworth Press.

Index

generation 133-4 parallel
distributive processing 120;
questioning 134-5; and responsibility 136-7; scoring 137; test
administration 138
concurrent validity 79-80
construct validity 80-1, 167
construction of tests: 39-51;
correction for guessing 48-50;
and factor analysis 120-7,
128-30; knowledge- and person-
based questionnaires 39-40;
norm-reference and criterion-
reference testing 43-7; objective
and open-ended tests 40-3;
psychological traits, true scores,
and internal test structure 58-9;
questionnaires 143-71; summing
of item scores 47-8
content validity 78, 166-7
continuous assessment 103-4
correction, for guessing in objective
knowledge-based tests 48-50
correlation 5
correlation coefficient 114-20
criterion-referenced testing 43-7
item analysis 57-8
Cronbach, L.J. 76-7
culture, and intelligence 10-11

Darlington, C. 97
Darwin, Charles 4, 7
Debra P. v. *Turlington* (1983) 46-7
Diana v. *California State Board of
Education* 100
discrimination, item 54-6, 57, 161

education: examinations 6, 8, 20;
alternative approaches 102-4;
graded tests 110-11; minimum
competency testing 45-7; profiles
107-10
Einhorn, H. 97
Elliot, C. 67, 133
employment, examinations 3, 102
equal opportunities legislation 91,
101
error: item 121; and reliability 75-6

ethics of intelligence testing 18-20
Eugenics movement 7-8
evolution 4
examinations: education 6, 8, 20,
102-4; employment 3, 102
'expert systems' 139-40
extrinsic test bias: 99-101; and
ideology 99; legal aspects 100-1
Eysenck, H.J. 8, 15, 80-2, 127
Eysenck Personality Inventory (EPI)
80-1, 82

face validity 78, 166
facility, item 53-4, 56-7, 160-1
factor analysis: 13, 59-61, 114-30;
and construction of tests 120-7,
128-30; correlation coefficient
114-20; criticisms 127-8; and
item error 121; number of
factors 124-7; rotation of factors
124-7
Ford, S.F. 92
formative assessment 103-4
function approach to psychometrics
26, 27-8, 31-8

GCE 103-4
GCSE 103
Galton, Sir Francis 4, 28
generalizability theory 76-7
genetics 9-10
Gipps, C. 65
Golden, C.J. 111
Golombok, Susan 130
Golombok Rust Inventory of
Marital State (GRIMS) 143-71
passim
Golombok Rust Inventory of Sexual
Satisfaction (GRISS) 106, 130
Gorsuch, R.L. 137
graded testing 110-11
Graduate Record Examination
(GRE) 101
graphical normalization 86, 87
Greg, W.R. 13
Griggs v. *Duke Power Co.* (1971)
32, 100
Gross, A.L. 98